"I used these ideas in class and had a wonderful day with my students."

Thank you so much!! I used these ideas in class and had a wonderful day with my students. As a first Year Relief Teacher I find this site invaluable in helping me become a better and more confident Teacher.

Jess (Take Control of the Noisy Class customer)

*   *   *

"It is very rewarding to see a teacher apply strategies from Rob's materials, then get excited as they see the 'magic' work."

"The materials have been right on target, students have benefitted as well as teachers. It is very rewarding to see a teacher apply strategies from Rob's materials, then get excited as they see the 'magic' work. Thank you for making my job easier and validating the experience."

Cheryl E. Le Fon (Take Control of the Noisy Class customer)

Connect With Your Students

How to Build Positive Teacher-Student Relationships - The #1 Secret to Effective Classroom Management

Needs-Focused Teaching Resource Book 5

Rob Plevin

www.needsfocusedteaching.com

About the Author

Rob Plevin is an ex-deputy head teacher and Special Education Teacher with the practical experience to help teachers in today's toughest classrooms.

No stranger to behaviour management issues, Rob was 'asked to leave' school as a teenager. Despite his rocky route through the education system he managed to follow his dream of becoming a teacher after spending several years working as an outdoor instructor, corporate trainer and youth worker for young people in crisis. Since then he has worked with challenging young people in residential settings, care units and tough schools and was most recently employed as Deputy Head at a PRU for children and teenagers with behaviour problems. He was identified as a key player in the team which turned the unit round from 'Special Measures'.

He now runs needsfocusedteaching.com, is the author of several books and presents training courses internationally for teachers, lecturers, parents and care workers on behaviour management & motivation. His live courses are frequently described as 'unforgettable' and he was rated as an 'outstanding' teacher by the UK's Office for Standards in Education.

Rob's courses and resources feature the Needs-Focused Approach™ – a very effective system for preventing and dealing with behaviour problems in which positive staff/student relationships are given highest priority.

To book Rob for INSET or to enquire about live training please visit the help desk at

www.needsfocusedteaching.com

Introduction

Free bonus materials & printable resources

This book, like the others in this series, is for teachers like you who want to connect and succeed with tough, hard-to-reach students in the shortest possible time. To help you do this, it comes complete with additional bonus material as well as printable resources to accompany the activities explained in the book.

 Wherever you see the '**resource icon**' in this book, head over to our website to get your free resources and accompanying printables,

Please visit:

http://needsfocusedteaching.com/kindle/connect/

About the Book

This is book #5 in my Needs-Focused Teaching Resource series. This collection of teaching books is my attempt to provide teachers with practical, fast-acting, tried-and-tested strategies and resources that work like magic in today's toughest schools. The novel, quirky ideas and methods form part of my Needs Focused Approach and have been tried and tested with hard-to-reach, reluctant learners of all ages, in more than 40 countries. Over the last 10 years or more they have been found to be highly effective in improving learning, raising achievement, building trusting relationships and creating positive learning environments.

Each book in this series includes a comprehensive suite of bonus materials and printable resources as I want to give you as much support as possible and for you to be delighted with your book purchase. Please be sure to download your bonus resources from my website here:

http://needsfocusedteaching.com/kindle/connect/

The Needs Focused Approach

The Needs-Focused Teaching System is explained fully in my main classroom management book, 'Take Control of the Noisy Class – From Chaos to Calm in 15 seconds'. It's available on Amazon in both Kindle and physical formats.

Briefly, this approach is based on Abraham Maslow's Hierarchy of Needs theory which suggests that human beings share a wide range of emotional and psychological needs – from the need to achieve through the need to contribute, to the need for love and a whole host of others in between.

By meeting these needs in the classroom teachers can effectively maximise student engagement while preventing behaviour problems which often arise due to feelings of boredom, frustration and alienation. We focus on just three broad groups - 'Empowerment' which includes things like recognition, freedom, autonomy, achievement, contribution, choice and competence; 'Fun' which includes curiosity, interest, growth and learning, adventure, amusement, surprise, variety; and finally the need to 'Belong' – to be accepted, valued, appreciated, needed, related to or connected with something beyond oneself.

The ideas and activities in this book will help you give your students a sense of belonging – by making them feel part of the classroom community, by strengthening peer relationships and by building positive, mutually respectful student-teacher bonds. They will help you empower your students by providing them with realistic chances to achieve and experience success, by giving them a degree of autonomy and choice and by ensuring their efforts are recognised and acknowledged. And they will help you improve motivation in lessons by providing opportunities to have fun.

Opening Remarks

I often start the relationship-building section of my classroom management workshops with the words *"If you can master this ONE topic, you need not listen to anything else I say today; this is the only behaviour management tool you'll ever really need."*

And then I get participants to try and guess what I'm referring to by telling the (true) story of a teacher who returned to teaching after a career break and found himself struggling to manage the behaviour of his students - largely because he had neglected to pay attention to this key area. He found himself being laughed at and ignored and many of his lessons were completely out of control.

I then point out that this same teacher happened to have co-authored a highly respected book on classroom management, was a qualified psychologist, a senior teacher with 15+ years' classroom experience and later became a university lecturer in teacher training.

This presents something of a conundrum. Here we have a very experienced and intelligent teacher who finds himself totally unable to control his students despite having written a comprehensive textbook on dealing with classroom behaviour problems. He knows all the theories, he's got all the skills and strategies and yet he can't get the kids to behave. What is going on? How can this be?

Well, the answer is simply that he had no relationship with his new cohort of students - he didn't know them and they didn't know him. And because they didn't know him they could neither trust him nor respect him. How can you really trust someone you don't know?

This teacher had returned to the classroom thinking that all the wonderful theories, acronyms and case studies he had carefully explained in his book would help him swiftly brush aside any of the classroom problems he was likely to encounter. But he had forgotten one of the most important principles of successful teaching – students will always respond more positively to a teacher they know, like and trust. (I should add that the author was quick to realise his error and promptly set about resolving his predicament. He began focusing heavily on his relationship with the students and saw an almost-immediate improvement in their attitudes and behaviour).

I get emails all the time from teachers who blame the system – the school, the setting, the building, the students, the parents, the lack of support from senior staff, the policies etc. for their inability to maintain an orderly classroom but these factors have no real relevance for the teacher who has a good relationship with his or her students. I've seen it too many times to doubt this - teachers with relationships at the core of their practice can go into virtually any classroom, in any school, and succeed with even the most belligerent, difficult students.

It's not rocket science, is it? It's obvious that kids will generally behave better and work harder for teachers they know, like and trust. And in this resource I'm going to show you some of the best, fast-acting ideas and strategies I know of for building positive relationships with hard-to-reach students and becoming the teacher they respect and value. When you apply these strategies in the way I'm going to show you too will see RAPID improvements in the way your students treat you and respond to you. That's why I really do believe this to be the #1 secret to effective classroom management.

You really can gain respect very quickly from tough students no matter how bad your situation is currently. You really can see miraculous transformations in terms of their attitudes towards you and you really can get them to respond more positively to your instructions. It's all possible when you focus on building positive relationships with them and this resource contains everything you need to be able to do so in record time.

Now, before we get into the ideas and concepts for building relationships there's an important question I need to address... 'Why bother with all this relationship-building stuff?'

When I introduce the notion of spending time getting to know students in our workshops a proportion of participants start to get all jumpy. They tell me they haven't got the time for this; their job is to teach students, not like them; they teach 300 students a week and could never get to know them all anyway; they have too much paperwork to do and it's unreasonable of me to add to their workload etc. etc.

I sympathise; I have been there too. I know how much pressure teachers are under and I also know how pompous trainers appear when they suggest such things. So my best answer to the 'why bother?' question is that doing this is actually going to save you time in the long run and it will make your job much, much easier and far more enjoyable. Let me share this quick story to explain why...

A few years ago I was talking with a friend of mine after delivering training at his school. He, (let's call him John), told me a story about one of the teachers at the school, (she can be called Janet for the purpose of this story and for the benefit of any Terry Wogan fans), who was struggling badly with one particular group of students; she just couldn't get them quiet.

John was Janet's head of department and he often had to pass through her room when she was teaching in order to get resources from the main store cupboard. He told me that on one particular day he happened to be passing through when Janet was teaching her most challenging group.

The students were literally out of control – screaming, shouting and totally ignoring Janet's cries to settle down. John didn't normally intervene unless asked to do so but he felt this situation was only going to get worse so he walked round the room speaking quietly to some of the students for a few minutes. Without the need to raise his voice, a hush gradually descended on the room and the students returned to their seats facing Janet; happy faces, ready to work.

John quietly left the room and went about the rest of his day without giving the incident a second thought.

At the end of the school day, when the students had left the premises, Janet caught John in the staffroom...

"John, how do you do that? How the hell do you manage to get that group so quiet so easily?" she asked. "They won't do anything I say and yet they settle straight away for you. I spend the whole lesson fighting with them. What do you do? What is it? What's the secret?"

I'm sure she didn't expect the reply he gave her. She wanted a magic bullet, a sure-fire strategy, a new way of speaking, a secret hand signal or a never-fail script to follow. But I hope she understood the power of what he said and I hope you do too, it's priceless. It is the single, most important tool any teacher can develop and it leads to an enviable level of respect from your most challenging students.

"I'll tell you exactly how I do it, there's no magic to it....

I know these kids. I've spent time with them. I go to support them playing football for the school at weekends, I chat with them in the corridor, I regularly speak to their parents on the telephone, I visit their homes, I've taken them on trips, I sit with them at lunch time. The door to my room is always open to them, they know they can come and chat when something's wrong and I make a point of catching up with them whenever I can."

I maintain, as my friend does, that there is no real 'secret' to successful classroom management other than making positive relationships the foundation of your overall approach.

With that said, let's get started with the 'Two Essential Factors for Building Positive Relationships FAST'...

The Two Essential Factors for Building Positive Relationships FAST

OK, we all know how important positive relationships with students are. When we go to Teacher Training College, we are told that we must have positive relationships with our students. When we are teaching books, they tell us that we MUST have positive relationships with our students, our colleagues tell us the same things, and deep down we all know that positive staff-student relationships are at the heart of good teaching.

But the big question is this...'how do we go about doing that?' I mean specifically. What are the exact steps that we should take in order to develop those bonds, in order to build that positive relationship? It's one thing to know that we should do something; it's another thing entirely actually doing it – especially when you don't really know how.

As a senior teacher in a small PRU (Pupil Referral Unit) some years ago I was well aware of this and spent a great deal of time trying to subtly encourage and advise other members of staff as to how they could best get on with our more challenging students.

And if I'm honest I found this extremely frustrating – I really struggled to boil down the essentials into an easy-to-follow format that my fellow teachers could effectively use.

Eventually I found that the simplest way of thinking of a relationship is as a kind of 'account' – a relationship account, a bit like a bank account. When we want to grow our money in a bank account we put more money in... and we get money back out in the form of interest. So, to make our money account grow we make deposits - and the more money we put in, the more we get back out. In other words, we have to give in order to receive.

With a relationship account it's much the same principle - the more we put in to the relationship account, the more we get back out. But we don't put money in (unless we're talking about the relationship with our own children), we make our deposits with something very different and much more valuable – we give ourselves – and we do it in two ways:

By showing the other person we <u>CARE</u> about them and by <u>COMMUNICATING FREQUENTLY</u> with them

If you think about the important relationships in your life – those with your spouse, your friends, your family – you will see that this is true. You simply cannot have a positive, flourishing relationship unless <u>communication</u> of some sort is taking place frequently. We are almost constantly connecting through speech (face to face, mobile, Skype etc.) and the written word (text, letters, email, social media etc.). And it is certain that both parties in a good relationship <u>care</u> about each other. We show we care by helping each other, doing favours, saying nice things, giving gifts, going to the in-laws' for lunch etc.

By concentrating on these two essential factors – showing we care and frequent communication - I believe we have the simplest possible formula for building relationships with our students and we're going to be exploring multiple ways of doing this throughout this manual. If you doubt the efficacy of this, let me tell you another story about someone who used these two factors as the main tool for building positive relationships in his sales career - with dramatic results.

Joe Girard, was a car salesman and earned the title 'World's Best Salesman'. As you can imagine, you have to sell a lot of cars to reach the title of best salesman in the world. Joe managed to do it a staggering 12 years in a row.

He attributes his success largely to the relationships he had with his customers, and the way he went about building relationships with those customers is utterly fascinating, yet remarkably simple. Basically, all he did was this: Whenever he met someone - in the street, in a shop, at a party, whatever - he would ask their name and address and enter them into his database. From that moment on, every month, these people would get a handwritten greetings card from Joe Girard. Inside the card would be a brief but warm message on the lines of *"Hey I was just thinking about you. All the best, Joe Girard"* or *"Hey! I hope everything's going great for you. Kind regards, Joe Girard."*

At his peak, Joe was sending out more than 14,000 hand written greetings cards every month - about 500 hand-written cards a day and at that point he was employing three staff just to help him write them! Now, you might be wondering why a salesman would bother sending out all those cards – particularly when there was no mention of selling anything in them. All he was doing was keeping in touch, sending a warm greeting to people he barely knew. But think about this... Most people change their car every few years. Who do you think was first in the minds of each of those 14,000 people when they next thought about replacing their vehicle?

You can see that Joe's formula for building relationships - communicating frequently with each person and then showing that he cared about them - matches ours perfectly. So let's find out how to apply these two essential factors to the classroom setting...

Essential Factor #1

Frequent Communication

As we've discussed, *all* relationships have frequent communication at their heart. You can't have a relationship unless communication is involved in some form so it's not surprising we often have poor relationships with our most challenging students – they're usually the last people we 'chat along nicely' with.

And often that's because talking with them is actually very difficult - getting them to open up and start communicating is the first hurdle. Striking up a conversation with your average, maladjusted 14 year old is difficult – especially when you don't know them very well.

It's a vicious circle; you can't get to know them until you have something to talk about and you have little to talk about with them until you get to know them better. The problem is <u>having something to talk about</u> so our first step in terms of communicating frequently with students is finding out their likes/dislikes, hobbies and passions - we have more chance of getting them to talk with us if we talk about something which actually interests them.

Clearly, once you know their passions you can easily strike up conversation with them - you have a subject to chat about which will interest and engage them. For example, if their favourite subject turns out to be 'mountain biking' you could:

- Ask their advice about new bikes, local tracks or related equipment (we all like to be able to show how knowledgeable we are about a subject, particularly if it's our favourite).

- Bring an old bike into school and ask them to help you fix it.

- Share stories you've seen on TV about mountain biking.

- Visit websites on mountain biking and share what you find

- Find old books/magazines or newspaper clippings and offer them as a something to look at in their spare time.

The following six ideas will help you discover your students' interests...

Six Ways to Discover Student Interests

'Find their interests' method #1:

Questions on the board

Try putting a simple question on the board at the end of the lesson:

"What are your three favourite hobbies?"

"If you had £20/$20 to spend which shop would you go in and what would you buy?" "What do you do on a Saturday?"

"What is your favourite film/TV program/type of music?

Etc.

Ask students to write their answers on a piece of paper with their name on and leave it in the suggestion box by the door on their way out.

Record Card Questionnaire

These questionnaires are a nice, non-invasive, under-the-radar way to uncover the hobbies, passions and interests of your students and once you do so your ability to start a conversation with them is virtually guaranteed. Everybody likes talking about their favourite subject.

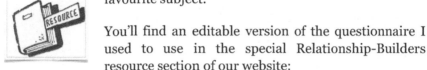

You'll find an editable version of the questionnaire I used to use in the special Relationship-Builders resource section of our website:

http://needsfocusedteaching.com/kindle/connect/

Thumb Ball

The Thumb Ball is a fun, low pressure way to get students opening up and interacting. When used correctly they provide a brilliant way to get students talking about themselves. Use it as a starter, energiser, 'getting-to-know-you' or Circle Time activity to stimulate peer relationships and discover student interests.

The basic principle is to throw the ball to a member of the group and get them to respond to one of the categories under their thumb when they catch it – hence the name.

Building your own Thumb Ball:

All you need is a soft sponge ball – 15-30cm in diameter (a vinyl-coated ball would be best for writing on but they are hard to source) – and a permanent marker pen. The following sets of words/phrases will give ideas for suitable categories to write on the ball.

Sample words/phrases for a 'Skills' ball:

Responsibility

Perseverance

Social skills

Belief in yourself

Consequences

Dedication

Qualifications

Gratitude

Planning

Goals

Reading

Relaxation

Emotional control

Listening

Keeping a cool head

Helping others

Sample words/phrases for a 'Conversation Starter' ball:

Animal sounds

Football teams

Cartoon characters

Noisy things

Round things

Things to take camping

Jewellery

Tools

Occupations

Types of furniture

Breeds of dog

Fancy dress costumes

Countries

Fairy tales

Most difficult things

Vehicles

Scariest thing

Things in the sky

NB// Ready-made Thumb Balls are available from www.ThumbBall.com

Prompts can be used by asking questions in the following ways:

How have you recently experienced/used (the <u>category</u>)? (e.g. *'How have you recently taken <u>responsibility</u>?'*)

How do you plan to experience/use (the <u>category</u>)? (e.g. *'How will you be taking <u>responsibility</u> soon?'*)

Can you praise someone else for using (the category)? (e.g. *'Have you noticed anyone else being responsible this week?'*)

What happens if someone uses/experiences (the category)? (e.g. *'What happens if everyone takes more/less responsibility?'*)

Which is more important (category 1) or (category 2)? (e.g. *'Which is more important, responsibility or relaxation? Why?'*)

Other Examples:

Category: "Fancy Dress Costumes"

First question...*"What was the last costume you wore?"*

Follow up questions... *"Why did you choose it?"*, *"Who else was at the party?"*, *"Did you have a good time?"* etc.

Category: "Things to take camping"

First question... *"You have ten seconds to list as many things as you can that you would take camping."*

Follow up questions...*"When did you last go camping?"*, *"Where would you like to go camping?"*, *"What do you like best about camping?"* etc.

Other ways to distribute the ball:

1. Individuals throw ball up in the air, catch and respond to prompt

2. Pairs pass Thumb Ball between them

3. Small and large groups in a circle pass Thumb Ball around in order

4. Small and large groups in a circle throw Thumb Ball randomly across circle

5. Throw 2 or 3 different Thumb Balls around a circle at the same time

Cooperative Cards

These work in much the same way as the Thumb Ball. Questions are written on each card and offered to students.

The student takes one and responds accordingly. These are also a good group activity – split students into groups of four and have them work through a selection of cards by themselves to build team spirit and encourage students to discover more about each other.

 You will find editable, ready-to-print 'Cooperative Cards' in the special Relationship-Builders resource section of our website:

http://needsfocusedteaching.com/kindle/connect/

Suggestion Box

Have a cardboard box on your desk and invite students at the end of a session to give you some information about their interests. *"On your way out please write your favourite hobby/team/band/sport etc. on a piece of paper with your name on and leave it in the box on my desk."*

Computer Time

Give students ten minutes of free time on the internet and monitor which sites they visit. (It is obviously assumed that measures are in place to prevent them from visiting sites they 'really' want to visit!)

Additional 'Find-their-interest' ideas:

You'll find more ways to discover their interests in the activities section of this book under the heading 'Getting-To-Know-You Activities'.

Ways to start conversations with students when they'd rather not talk with you...

OK, we've covered some ways to find out your students' interests but as well as knowing their interests you also need a way of <u>starting</u> the conversation with them up your sleeve too. Getting adolescents to start talking to you can be very uncomfortable - it often seems they would much rather do anything but talk to you. For that reason we need - a 'way-in' - and that's exactly what I'm going to give you now... six of them in fact.

'Way-in' #1:

Ask them for advice

When people are given the chance to express their opinions it shows that you value them and what they have to say. It's empowering – people like to feel important and valued. Ask your students questions that allow them to express their interests and ideas - things they know about. Girls love to give advice on fashion, hair styles, make up, jewellery, shops etc. and tend to be experts on soaps on TV. Boys like to give advice on computer games, sports and pretty much anything practical or technical.

So if you're stuck for something to say to your students start by asking their advice. You might ask some of the girls for their opinion on what you should wear for an upcoming party or suggesting a suitable CD for your own child's birthday. You might ask for a run-down of the latest happenings on the current hot soap or ask them a decent shop to buy a new bag for you or your spouse. If you're trying to strike up a conversation with a boy try getting him to help you with something of a practical nature. I once took my mountain bike into school with me and asked three of my new students to help me fit some parts at lunch time. Prior to this day I had really struggled to break the ice with these boys but we never looked back after our 'cycle workshop' session – it was a great way to start a conversation and start building a relationship with them.

Tip: When it comes to talking about personal matters make sure it is their advice you're asking for – not their opinion. Asking a student what they think of your new hairstyle may set you up for ridicule while asking them to suggest a decent hairdresser probably won't.

'Way-in' #2:

Ask a favour – 'The Franklin Effect'

When we think about ways to build bonds with people we intuitively think along the lines of doing something nice for them or caring about them – as per our second 'Essential Strategy'. The 18th century politician Benjamin Franklin found an alternative, counter-intuitive approach which can be equally, if not more, effective in certain situations: asking favours.

To cut a long story very short, Franklin had been trying to connect with a fellow politician for some time but just wasn't able to; the other man wanted nothing at all to do with him. Franklin knew that this man happened to have a certain rare book in his personal library and he asked if he could borrow it from him. Surprisingly, the man's attitude towards Franklin changed completely from that moment on…

"When we next met in the House, he spoke to me (which he had never done before), and with great civility; and he ever after manifested a readiness to serve me on all occasions."

Franklin attributed this to a simple principle –

- "If you want to increase the likelihood of someone liking you, get them to do you a favour."

I found this in a fascinating book called ':59 Seconds' by Professor Richard Wiseman and if you think about it, it makes perfect sense – when you do someone a favour it draws you towards them; helping people gives us a sense of being needed or wanted, it feels good, there is joy in giving.

If you want to employ the 'Franklin Effect' ask a troublesome student to help you sort something out with your car, , decorate your house, do your ironing…It does make sense – when you help someone out or do something positive for them you naturally feel a connection with them; contribution feels good,

So, next time you're trying to make a connection and find a way in with a student, remember the Franklin Effect. You could ask them to help you sort a problem with your laptop, carry some heavy equipment, choose an outfit for an upcoming party, pick a CD for your own child's birthday, help design a wall display, decorate your house, do your ironing…

Use WRITTEN communication

Don't underestimate this – it can be a very powerful way of connecting with some students – particularly those who are reluctant to talk face to face. There are all kinds of ways of using the written word to build relationships. Here are a few you could try:

<u>Notes</u>:

Notes can be hand-written or typed and can be a great, non-threatening way to address concerns:

<u>Example 1</u>

Dear...

The work you did in class today was excellent. It's so nice to see you putting in more effort and you really can do well when you try can't you? Come to think of it, you could do even better if you would get your homework in on time. Just in case you didn't write it down, tonight's homework is...

If you need any help on it, make sure you see me before going home tonight so that we can make sure you do a good job on it. Let's make it 'your best ever homework'! I'll look forward to seeing you hand it to me on Wednesday. Have fun...

<u>Example 2</u>

> Dear...
>
> It was wonderful to see you in class today. The lesson always has a livelier atmosphere when you're around. For that reason it would be nice to see more of you. Can you make sure that you're in class on time tomorrow please so that I don't get worried about you? Remember, lessons start at 9.10am sharp. See you in the morning...

Cards:

- •Birthday cards: Go a step further than saying 'Happy Birthday'. Make them feel special by sending a card (posting it home gets bonus points).

- •'Thank You' cards: When they do something right/good, saying 'thank you' shows you've noticed and are grateful. Giving them a card in an envelope says much more.

Post-It Notes:

Marking books is a great chance to build relationships because the comments often develop into private conversations. By using post-it notes or even writing directly in their books you can ask them questions, send them good wishes, congratulate them on an achievement, tell them jokes and give feedback of all kinds. These private little dialogues all go towards conveying the message that you care about and value them.

Way-in #4:

Give sincere compliments

Research has shown that when a person gives a compliment, the person who has been complimented later describes that person as taller, slimmer and younger than they really are. So, not only are compliments a great way to improve relationships and build a more positive classroom… giving them has the added bonus of making you lose weight, gain height and look younger!

On a more serious note, compliments (when they're used in the way I've explained below) are also an effective way to start a conversation with students when you either don't know them very well or are struggling to find something positive to say to them.

The problem with compliments is that they are often dismissed by the recipient. This might be because they don't really 'believe' the comment or perhaps they feel it is an attempt to manipulate them. Whatever the reason, it results in comments being rejected a bit like this…

"I like your shoes"

"What, these? This is just an old pair."

And this is one reason why most of us are so bad at giving compliments – we think the other person won't believe what we say or will think we're just after something. To get over this hurdle, (and take advantage of the huge benefits compliments have to offer us in our relationship-building quest), we need to learn how to make them more believable.

We can do that by adding just three pieces of information…

1. **Use the person's name to make it more personal**

2. **Give credibility by telling them 'why'**

3. **Finish with an open-ended question – Why did you choose it? How did you learn it? etc.**

"Hey Jonny (name)I like your shoes. My son would love a pair like that for his interview next week (why you like them). Did you buy them round here? (question)"

"Hey Jonny, I hear you played very well in the match on Saturday. Mr Smith said you were very good in defence. What were the other team like?"

Don't those compliments sound more credible?

Way-In #5:

'Referral Marketing'

Businesses use referral marketing all the time; they rely on endorsements and recommendations from related businesses to spread the word about their products and services to their customers. The fact that the related business already has an established relationship with their customers means that a referral is usually positively received. So the principle here is to 'piggyback' on an established relationship between a student and another teacher. If you are struggling to make connections with a particular student but you know of a colleague who gets on very well with them, the idea is simply to get your colleague to introduce you to the student. As long as the student respects your colleague and gets on well with them, a joint meeting can be set up where the three of you can sit down and discuss ways in which you and the student can successfully move forward. Barriers normally come down after this initial meeting.

Essential Factor #2:

Showing That You CARE

The second of our key relationship-building factors is showing students that you value them and care about them. The following ideas should help...

'Show you care' method #1:

Have MASSIVE expectations

In the same way that Greek sculptor, Pygmalion's, high expectations became a self-fulfilling prophecy and turned a lifeless statue into a beautiful living being, the thoughts and beliefs we hold about our students can have quite dramatic effects on them.

In 1968 Rosenthal & Jacobson conducted a study involved giving a group of teachers some false information about the learning potential of a group of students in a San Francisco elementary school. The teachers were told that some of the students had been tested and found to be experiencing rapid intellectual growth whereas, in actual fact, the students had been selected at random. At the end of the experiment some of the targeted students - especially those in grades one and two – performed better in tests than other students of similar ability, and superior to what would have been expected if they'd had no intervention. Rosenthal & Jacobson concluded that teacher expectations can have a positive impact in the classroom because students' achievements come to reflect those expectations.

To take advantage of this phenomenon, start by giving your students positive labels – try referring to them all (even the 'really' challenging ones) as 'top students', 'excellent workers' or your 'favourites' and you might find it makes them feel more positively about themselves... and behave accordingly.

Constantly remind them that they ARE capable, they ARE good role models, they ARE likeable, they ARE wonderful, they ARE helpful, they ARE worthy of success and that they CAN improve providing they are willing to put in the effort. Children need to know that someone in authority believes in them and they need to feel that people care about them, understand them and like them. When you do this – when you really put effort into it - you will find your students respond differently towards you. Give to receive, remember.

'Show you care' method #2:

Give or lend them something special

How many times does your most challenging student forget to bring a pen to the lesson? Instead of handing them a chewed old Bic pen from the 'pen graveyard' why not use this as an opportunity to build the vital teacher/student relationship? Lending them a tatty, chewed, broken cheap pen says *"I don't think very much of you - I don't trust you enough to give you a decent pen and I don't think you deserve one."* but taking them to one side and saying *"this pen was a gift from my son. I'm going to trust you with it because I want you to learn how to look after things and I want you to write well today"* gives an entirely different message.

Students respond to us in the way they feel they're being treated – treat them with contempt and they will respond with indignation. Treating them with respect and giving them the clear message that you trust them and value them will evoke positive feelings and an entirely different reaction.

Perform Acts of Random Kindness

If you've seen the film Evan Almighty (a funny and surprisingly good film with some powerful messages) you'll know that the word ARK (as in 'Noah's Ark') stands for Acts of Random Kindness.

The idea here is to try performing random acts of service or appreciation for your students to make them feel special... and then stand back and watch what happens. You can increase the effects by adding an encouraging note for them to 'Pay it Forward' (another great film) to other students. We've just mentioned one such act above – lending or giving them a special.object of some sort - but this can be extended to giving additional time or 'doing' something special for a student who would benefit.

This is an excellent way to change a students' negative attitudes and can quickly create a more caring and nurturing environment. One of the greatest ways to increase self-esteem is to serve, help or express sincere appreciation to another person because one of our powerful 'needs' is the need to contribute or actually feel needed. This is the perfect way to satisfy that need.

Here's an example of this which targets the whole group rather than individual students; it won't appeal to everyone reading this but it's very powerful none the less... The idea is to go out of your way to be of total service to your class for a lesson or part thereof. Treat each student as if they were a high paying guest in a top restaurant – greet them politely by name at the door, seat them and provide them with an unexpected gift of a pen or other equipment and the offer to move seats if they are uncomfortable. Have soft music playing in the background and, while they are engaged in a nice activity, wait on them with soft drinks and a smorgasbord of sweets to choose from, presented on a cake stand, of course.

You could even dress up for the occasion and drape a wine waiter's towel over your arm. This isn't a strategy for every lesson, nor for every group you teach but as an impromptu way of saying 'thank you' to a group who have made positive changes or an attempt to break the mood state of a difficult group it takes some beating.

'Show you care' method #4:

Offer support

I remember one young 15 year old lad in a class I was covering many years ago whose behaviour truly pushed the envelope of unmanageability. The first lesson I had with him was a full-on battle of wits from bell to bell – he just would not settle, would not engage and was intent on wrecking the entire lesson.

I caught him next lesson at the door and asked him to wait with me while the other students went in. He thought he was going to get a rollicking for last lesson's performance and was rather taken aback when I said:

"You know what Jake? Last lesson I couldn't help feeling there was something wrong; you didn't seem happy at all. I don't want you coming to my lessons and having a bad time, I don't want to be on your case having a go at you." I smiled at him and he looked up at me as I continued. *"My lessons are supposed to be useful to you; I want you to get something out of them. Can you tell me what I can do to make it better for you please?"*

There was a long pause as he tried to make sense of what I was saying. Then he opened up, as if I'd turned a tap on. He began to tell me how he couldn't see the board, how he couldn't read very well and was supposed to wear glasses, how other students made fun of him if he did, and how he didn't understand most of what was going on. His behaviour was the classic result of some of the de-motivators mentioned in one of my other books – Motivate the Noisy Class – chiefly 'fear of failure' and 'inadequacy'

We had to cut our conversation short so that I could get in to start the lesson but those few moments outside the classroom were the beginning of a very different relationship between Jake and me.

He now saw me as someone who was there to help him and I saw him as a young boy who needed my help. I made a few changes to accommodate his weaknesses and gave him some extra support - and his behaviour miraculously changed overnight. He arrived to lessons with a smile and his hand shot up almost every time I asked a question. The effort he now put into his work was unbelievable.

'Show you care' method #5:

Give them responsibilities

Often, our most challenging students are those with the greatest leadership potential; their behaviour is driven by a quest for attention and power and their strong personalities make them popular ring leaders. Giving them a responsibility is very fulfilling for them and saves them trying to gain notoriety in less appropriate ways. It also gives you, the teacher, very useful classroom allies.

Responsibility can take many forms – from being in charge of certain equipment through to monitoring and supporting more vulnerable members of the class (such as victims of bullying), keeping a group's noise levels at acceptable levels or allowing students the opportunity to grade their own work and choose lesson activities.

Ideas for roles/areas of responsibility could include:

- **Gofer** – a student selected to run errands (Go for this, go for that)

- **Board monitor** – a student responsible for cleaning the board and ensuring the surrounding area is tidy

- **Scribe** - if you like to have your lesson objective and lesson instructions written up at the start of the lesson, or this student will do it for you.

- **Gardner** – responsible for upkeep of indoor plants in the classroom

- **Equipment monitor** – responsible for keeping equipment trays tidy and complete

- **Noise controllers** – responsible for maintaining orderly working environment

- **Motivators** – responsible for encouraging slow workers

- **Registration monitor** – responsible for taking the register

Oh, in case you're wondering, the cartoon is a picture of some 'Shusshers'. These loyal and helpful souls are hand-picked on our live courses because they are highly skilled at 'shusshing' the rest of the participants when they make too much noise. I think the 'Shusshers' quite like it, everyone else thinks it's quite amusing and the trainer gets to save his/her voice for another day. Everyone's a winner with responsibilities.

'Show you care' method #6:

Give them Choices

One of the least empowering strategies a teacher can use is to constantly dictate and give orders in the classroom. Students get fed up of being told what to do and not being allowed to exercise free choice. Choice gives students a feeling of autonomy and freedom and shows you care and understand enough about them to know that they will appreciate different options.

For example, instead of dictating that they complete a single designated task, try giving them a limited choice in the form of a voting slip (a verbal discussion can sometimes lead to arguments and a vote is more fun) written out as follows...

Which of the following tasks would you prefer?

a) Produce a mind-map on........

b) Produce a newspaper report on.......

c) Work as a group to find a solution to......

d) Complete exercise.........

The activity with the most votes wins and by taking part in this vote you agree to take part in the chosen activity without argument.

'Show you care' method #7:

Send cards

Cards, notes and letters show much more consideration and appreciation than words. If it's their birthday, go a step further than saying 'Happy Birthday' – make them feel special and give them a card. (Physically posting it home gets you bonus points).

If they are ill, go a step further than marking them absent on the register – send a 'Get Well' card. And when they try particularly hard or do something especially nice, why not give them a 'Thank You' card?

Set challenges

Challenges can be set for individual students or for a whole group and they are a great way to show you want them to do well and that you're willing to put in a little extra time and effort to help them do so...

"People looking at your past scores will assume you're going to get a C in this next test. How about we put a plan together to prove them wrong?"

"In the staff meeting this morning all the staff were told that not one class has achieved 100% attendance for a whole term. How about we work together to prove them all wrong?"

Finally, challenges can also be used just to add a bit of fun to the curriculum:

"I'm betting there isn't a person in this room who can eat four dried crackers in under one minute!"

My favourite A-level Biology teacher set that last challenge to us one day at the start of a module on digestion to illustrate the fact that the breakdown of food starts with the action of saliva and chewing. It was messy and chaotic and I still smile when I think about it – more than twenty five years later!

Celebrate successes

Take opportunities to draw special attention to student successes and achievements, whether it be an individual or a group effort. Success can come in many guises – class work, homework, out of school behaviour, acts of kindness, good manners, sporting triumphs, winning X-Factor to name but a few. Bring treats, a cake, have a party, let them listen to music, or have some other reward on offer that shows you recognise their efforts.

'Show you care' method #10:

Show understanding (With the 'Blue's Card')

Tell the class that you realise that life can be challenging at home, school or with peers and that you are aware how life can throw up problems for young people. This shows empathy and respect for their challenges and that you care about their personal lives.

To take this a step further, give out 'Blues Cards' (a laminated blue piece of credit-card sized card) to each of your students:

BLUES CARD

This is your 'blues' card. Whenever you get 'the blues' you can trade your card by cashing it in for a treat. You get one card per term/month/week so use it wisely. It's just to show I'm aware of the issues you face.

'Treats' could include a one-day time extension for homework submission, a 10% boost to a test score, a pass for forgetting to bring equipment, a snack, 10 minutes on computer, a 10 minute walk outside, a 1:1 meeting with the school counsellor etc.

Give something back... together

Have students work together on a service project of some kind. The project should be focused on supporting and building up the community (e.g. gather clothes for the homeless, food donations, planting trees, litter removal, spending time with old people or those less fortunate etc.). Bonds can be built and strengthened very quickly during such projects, with everyone (including the teacher) working towards a worthwhile goal.

When students learn to turn outward in service we often see several positive benefits including: less depression, increased gratitude, self-esteem and motivation as well as a transformation in terms of behaviour.

'Show you care' method #12:

Let them grade you

Tell the students that your job is to help them succeed. In effect, you work for them which makes them your boss! That means they should be able to grade you in terms of your performance in teaching and helping them.

Explain to them the criteria for getting an 'A' grade as a student, and then ask them to give you their criteria for getting an 'A' grade as their teacher. Write their suggestions down and pin them up next to the board. Ask them to grade your work at various times, perhaps the end of each lesson or at least once a week. Students should be encouraged to give you constructive feedback along the way or to give you a score at the end of a lesson.

Give them extra time

Break times and lunch times are a fantastic relationship-building opportunity. A friend and teaching colleague of mine made a point of never spending his free time in school in the staffroom. Instead he spent break times and lunch times in his room with his door always open. Students came in to play chess and board games or just to chat and he rarely, if ever, had a problem with classroom management. His reputation as being 'there' for the students had spread throughout the whole school and they all knew him to be kind and approachable. He was greatly respected for that – even by the toughest students in the school.

'Show you care' method #14:

Have Post-It® conversations

Marking work can be a chore but it's also another opportunity to connect; to strengthen bonds or to initiate communication with students who don't like talking face to face.

For example: I placed a note in the work file of a boy who was visiting his father for the first time in several months. He was apprehensive about the visit so the "Good luck on Saturday" message I placed was just a quick, personal way of giving him a bit of support. Often students respond to written comments by writing replies and a 'Post-It® Conversation' develops - as does the relationship.

Here's another example along the same lines. It's part of a post I found on a forum several years ago from a parent who was very worried about her fragile, withdrawn young daughter, Holly, who was starting at a new school...

We waited anxiously for her to return home that day and asked her the inevitable question: *"What do you think of your new teacher?"*

"Oh, she seems pretty nice. Her name's Miss Daniels. She laughs and smiles a lot and she said she liked my new shoes."

Each day that week, Holly shared tales of Miss Daniels. She seemed to be enjoying school again. She smiled at supper and she laughed when getting dressed for school. She ran excitedly to the school bus. We were cautiously optimistic.

Friday evening, Holly went to her room to do her homework. Within five minutes she ran to the kitchen, beaming.

"Look Daddy," she said. *"Look what Miss Daniels sneaked into my book."*

Miss Daniels had secretly placed a note between the pages so it fell into Holly's lap when she opened the book. It read:

"You had a great first week Holly. I think this will be a good year for both of us. See you Monday.

Miss Daniels

"PS I love your shoes!"

Maybe she left notes like that for every child in the class but the point was that it made our fragile little girl feel special and it helped turn her around."

'Show you care' method #15:

Teach them new skills

We can show caring for a student by empowering them with skills to overcome their difficulties. I often use the example of a student who seldom, if ever, hands in homework. Does ranting at them make them correct their behaviour and do the required work? Could it be that the lack of effort is intensified by a lack of skills rather than pure belligerence?

Spending some time teaching this student some time management skills will show a deeper level of caring than a detention ever could and may even help them get their homework in on time.

Students who frequently break rules and seem unwilling to follow rules need support and education as much as they do discipline. Constantly and repeatedly punishing them for things they do wrong does not address the underlying issue – it doesn't show them how to do it right. Training them as mediators and 'buddies' to other students, for example, can help them see their own problems in a different light and can lead to startling behaviour change. As well as that, it often leads to a deep connection to the member of staff who takes the time and effort to reach out to help them.

'Show you care' method #16:

Take time to learn their names

This has to be done as soon as possible; not only does it make classroom time much easier to manage, a student's name is also the most important word they hear. I'm saddened when I think back to the students whose names I hadn't managed or bothered to learn in my classes. As the year drew to a close there were still students I was referring to as 'you' with a pointed finger. What message does that give? "You're not important enough for me to bother learning your name." It's quite shocking and disheartening when you look at it like that. Here are some ways to make sure you never make the same mistake...

5 Techniques for Learning Names Quickly

i. Name Chain

Ask each student in turn to share his/her name and the names of people who have already introduced themselves. E.g. Person 1 says their name, person 2 then gives the first person's name as well as their own name and so on. As the chain becomes longer there will be more names to remember but they will have been repeated more often.

Extra: Turn it into an alliterative chain by asking each student to use an adjective before their name that begins with the same letter. E.g. *'This is Lucky Lee and my name is Rowdy Rob".*

ii. Memorable Pictures

This is my favourite and is the one I use most often working with new groups.

You can learn a class of 40 names in one lesson – it's all just a matter of making time to learn the names and concentrating for a few minutes at a time on this single task.

The principle behind this is that it is easier to remember pictures than words and once you get into the habit of doing this you'll be amazed how powerful it is. Start by drawing a seating plan – a quick sketch of the seating layout in the room with enough space to write each student's name in the picture of their seat.

Give the students a simple and enjoyable ten minute task – some brain-teasers or questionnaires which will occupy them without needing your assistance or attention. You want them quiet for ten minutes. Go round the class introducing yourself, checking their names off the register and adding their names to the seating plan.

Once that's done the fun starts. Whilst the students are working, take a name from the seating plan and find the individual in the sea of nameless heads. All you do now is link a crazy picture with their name in your head. It should take no more than thirty seconds per student and the crazier the picture the better.

For example, if a child's name is Robert, in my mind I might put them behind bars or in hand-cuffs as a 'robber'. Then I'd spend 30 seconds concentrating on their face and the new image - once you cement that image in your mind, it's hard to forget their name. Really simple, really works.

iii)Name Toss

Have class members stand in a circle with one person holding a soft ball, bean bag or similar object. The student holding the object states their name and then throws it to another member in the circle. The 'catcher' then gives their name as they throw it to someone else. This is repeated until everyone has introduced themselves (you might give them a sticker once they've done this so that everyone can see who has been asked and who hasn't.

Next, ask one of the students to say the name of another group member and then throw the object to this person. The catcher then repeats the name of the person who threw them the object and says the name of another group member before throwing the object to this person. And so on.

iv.Name Bingo

Prepare a blank Bingo form – 3x3 squares for groups of less than ten, 5x5 for groups of 25 or less, 6x6 for groups of 36 or less etc.

Get the group to mill around the room, meet each other and exchange names. Have them write the name of each person they meet in a separate square on their Bingo form. Tell them to put a 'zero' in all the squares that are unused at the end of the 'meeting' session.

Put everyone's name on a separate piece of paper in a hat and as the hat is passed round the group each person takes a turn of drawing one name out and reading the name out loud.

Everyone crosses off the name on their form as it is read out and yells 'Bingo!' whenever they get 4, 5 or 6 squares in a row (depending on the group size and number of squares on their form). Everyone will get Bingo several times and everyone is involved throughout.

v) Personalized Name Tags

Provide materials so that each student can develop a name tag that uses any of the following:

- A picture of a hobby, interest or favourite object

- A personal logo

- A coat of arms

- A collage of magazine pictures

Have a name-badge-building session and encourage students to display them for the first few days of term or hand each member of the group a tag belonging to someone else and ask them to mix and mingle until they've found the owner of the tag.

Take interest in their lives

Call out on Monday morning *"Who had a good weekend?"* Then ask follow up questions to get students to share what they did.

A Friday question might be *"Who is looking forward to the weekend? Why?"*

Hang a calendar in your room that the students can write activities and announcements on. (Examples: concert, team trials, meetings etc.)

Have a notice board where students can share photographs of the hobbies and out-of-school activities.

Celebrate birthdays

Send a class card to the birthday student.

As a class sing "Happy Birthday" to the birthday student.

Allow the birthday student to bring in a little snack to share.

Allow the birthday student to leave first/turn in homework a day late.

Provide a 'lucky dip' for birthday students with small gifts wrapped up.

Eat together

Humans bond over food. Celebrate the end of term, units, test periods etc. with a special snack meal and encourage students to bring in a food donation to share. From time to time join students for lunch in the school cafeteria.

Use lots of praise (when it is justified)

As a relationship-building strategy, genuine praise takes some beating. After all, everyone likes to feel appreciated and to have their efforts acknowledged. But the watchword here is 'genuine' – nothing will ruin your attempts to build trust and respect among your students faster than false commendation – kids are quick to spot an adult who is just trying to manipulate them. If you find it difficult to find reasons to praise students or if you're worried you sound false when you attempt to pay a compliment for a relatively minor improvement , (and don't worry – the many workshops I've ran on this topic would suggest most teachers struggle with this), you'll find the following tips very helpful...

Making praise more effective

i) Praise effort rather than achievement

Praise students for their effort alone if they have shown more interest in the challenge of a task and seem more focused on the taking part, rather than the outcome of it and how their results might compare to those of other students. *"You've tried so hard, you've really showed determination there"*.

By focusing on effort rather than achievement we can praise a student even if they fail - and that's very important. Waiting for a child to complete a task before praising them means missing out on untold opportunities to encourage them along the way. If a friend was dieting you wouldn't wait until they had reached their target weight before making positive comments, would you? You'd help them along the way with encouragement, because acknowledging their effort helps them stick in and persevere and, importantly, can help them overcome or avoid frustration. *"Jason you are working so well on this. What you've done so far is spot on, keep it up."*

ii) Avoid personal judgements

Rather than judging students by telling them what we think of their efforts we should be encouraging them to reflect on their own efforts. The following statements illustrate my meaning:

"I think you've done a great job" is a judgement which encourages the student to be dependent on the view of the teacher whereas *"You've done a great job"* encourages independence and self motivation.

Similarly, "I really like what you've done here" could be phrased as "You should be proud of what you've done here" and "You're my best student" could be phrased as "You work really hard in this class."

iii) Be aware that praise is often more effective on a 1:1 basis

Some students (a surprisingly large proportion) don't like receiving praise in front of other people. For whatever reason – some just can't accept compliments very well – so you have more chance of your praise being well-received if you give it out of earshot of the rest of the students. Catch them on the way out of the door, speak to them before the lesson in the corridor or call them over to a quiet corner of the room. Praise is much more sincere when it's a private affair.

iv) Make it specific

When you praise a child you make them feel your appreciation by telling them exactly WHAT they did and WHY it was good. True praise comes from genuinely noticing when they put effort into something or have managed to complete something they wouldn't normally manage. Giving thoughtful attention to a student's work or efforts demonstrates that you recognise their work or improved behaviour.

"Paul, stand back and look at what you've done... this is a fantastic portrait! What is really impressive is the way you've made that eye come to life by showing the light reflecting here. That really makes it come alive!"

"Paul, you've done so well. You've sat quietly for the last 10 minutes and got on with your work. That's great because I've been able to go and help other students and I haven't needed to shout at you. Well done!"

v) Prepare a bank of praise statements

It is hard sometimes finding things about which to praise students beyond the classic 'well done' and 'that's really good' and yet this strategy is so powerful that it can't be used as an excuse not to do it. One method we have found useful on live courses is to get participants to create their own bank of suitable comment starters like this:

1. *"I find it really helpful when you..."*

2. *"There are some days when someone does something which totally surprises me..."*

3. *"I know you struggle with... but what you have done there is superb."*

4. *"What are you like at accepting compliments? I know it can go to people's heads but I've got to say this..."*

5. *"Okay stop please, everyone, I need to say this. There are three people who deserve special mention for..."*

6. *"I just want you to know that when you put effort in like that it makes my job worthwhile."*

7. *"I know this hasn't been easy for you so I want you to know I'm doubly impressed about..."*

vi) Make them reflect on their efforts

Some people lavish praise on students for literally anything and everything in the hope that a torrent of positive words will raise their self-esteem and motivate them.

"Wow Jonny, you've finished yet another piece of work!"

Sometimes it's better to hang back with the constant compliments and just ask students to stop and think about their efforts. By doing so we encourage them to recognise and evaluate the positive feelings associated with positive action. And hopefully, if they enjoy these feelings, there is more chance they will want to repeat the actions – for themselves, and not just to please someone else.

"Hey Jonny... how does it feel to be getting all this work done today?"

Three Powerful Praise Strategies You Might Not Be Aware of...

In addition to straightforward positive comments, here are two more very powerful praise strategies you might not have used too often...

Powerful Praise Strategy #1: Ego praise

This is a great way to acknowledge a student's strengths, abilities and efforts indirectly - without saying anything to them directly. Some students, as we know, find it difficult to accept praise directly – this gets round the problem.

"Go and ask Jonathan about it – he's picked this up very quickly."

"Go and watch Alan for a minute – he's brilliant at this and you can learn a lot from him."

(Both statements would be spoken just loud enough for Jonathan and Alan to hear).

Powerful Praise Strategy #2: Stealth praise

This is another type of indirect praise (and don't worry, it doesn't involve sneaking around in a black balaclava). This time, you report the student's efforts and abilities to another member of staff just within earshot of the student, as if you're not aware they are listening. Students love to discover that teachers talk positively about them:

"Did you see what Alan did this morning Mr Smith? Honestly, I can't believe how hard that lad is trying; what a turn-around."

And here's one more praise strategy you'll almost certainly know about but may have overlooked (it is incredibly powerful)...

Powerful Praise Strategy #3: Written Praise

Sending a short, positive letter home can transform a previously negative child - literally overnight - into one who is motivated and eager to please. This is also one method that works well even with older students, right up to age 16 and beyond. And it is very effective for students who don't accept public praise very well - a letter home means their friends will never find out!

Letters home can be 'quick-notes' or more formal, traditional letters on school headed paper. You can send out simple postcards for odd pieces of particularly good work or award 'extra special' letters in response to sustained effort.

'Show you care' method #21:

The Staffroom Praise Board

This is a whole-school approach to building a positive atmosphere and positive relationships between staff and students. Understandably, individual students' efforts often get overlooked – particularly in a large setting. This strategy ensures that even the smallest improvements made by a particular student are noticed and acknowledged by EVERY member of staff.

Directions:

1. Assign an area of wall in the staffroom for the praise board. There should be room for five to ten A4 sheets and it should be an area which staff will see whenever they enter the staffroom.

2. Each week, students are nominated for a place on the praise board (they aren't told about this). Staff put forward a student and give reasons for their nomination. After a vote, a photo of each chosen student is put on the board together with a brief summary of why they have been chosen.

3. The idea is that every member of staff will see this board regularly throughout the course of the week. When they next see one of the students from the board – either in the classroom, in the dinner queue or out on the yard - they can mention how impressed they are with the student's achievement. Over the space of a week, a student will receive a huge amount of positive, and often much-needed, reinforcement with several members of staff acknowledging the same achievement.

"Hey Jonny, I hear you were very good in maths this week. Well done mate, keep it up!"

"Damien! A little bird told me you managed to get through a whole day without being sent out of a single lesson. Brilliant! Isn't it better when you're not getting detention every day?"

'Show you care' method #22:

Have meaningful conversations

There are different levels of conversation and the level at which we communicate with our students will dictate how fast our relationships with them develop.

In a 'communication levels' pyramid, the most basic level (level 1- the base of the pyramid) of communication is the 'Gossip Zone'. This is the area of playground chatter and banter. It's where people are idly passing on information without knowing much about the source or the truth behind what they are saying. Much of what is communicated in this zone is just regurgitated without thought. Communicating at this level just fills time and is neither meaningful nor memorable.

At level 2 (The next layer up) we talk about facts and we give out information. This is the area where a lot of teaching takes place because you are giving information which has more substance to it. Discussions take place here and it is also the level at which we give and receive advice.

Finally, we have level 3 (The top of the pyramid) where emotions and feelings are included. Inspirational leaders communicate on this level - it is where <u>deep</u> connections are made. Relationships can develop very quickly when communication and interaction involves feelings and emotions. Interestingly, a lot of people struggle to communicate at this level because it is a risky place to be; it's a place where you reveal more of your true self - your true feelings, beliefs and values – and the threat of having these judged or challenged can be very daunting.

To include more interaction at this level with your students try to bring positive emotions into the classroom whenever possible and take advantage of opportunities to laugh and joke with them – obviously without being unprofessional. Arrange occasional discussions and activities around social and environmental issues which stir up their emotions - encourage them to share their feelings (and share yours too) on issues raised.

Also remember that when you're dealing with a student who is wound up and in a raw state emotionally, there is a golden opportunity to strike bonds with them. Showing support and kindness and helping them move from a negative to a more positive condition anchors you as a positive, stable influence in their lives – and someone they will naturally respect.

'Show you care' method #23:

Take the Relationship Challenge

On some of our live courses we introduce an activity called the 'Relationship Challenge'. Briefly, this involves making a definite commitment to improve relationships with any particularly hard to reach students who are causing you difficulties.

The idea is that you totally focus on improving your relationship with just one student at a time. That's not to say you ignore the others, but that you make more of an effort with this one student.

So, the idea is to aim to spend just ONE MINUTE a day for twenty days (four working weeks) engaged in relationship-building conversation with this particular student – and then see how your relationship with them changes. If you find yourself doing more, even better; the target is just one minute, more than that is a bonus. Everyone can manage one minute.

Just to clarify, 'relationship-building conversation' doesn't mean ordering them to sit properly in lessons or asking them why their homework hasn't been handed in; it's in addition to normal, day to day, instructional conversation. You can talk about anything at all – TV, music, football scores, asking them where they bought their cool new shoes, anything including their hobbies and interests. If you find this difficult remember to try any of the 'Way-In' conversation starters explained above.

One minute isn't a huge amount of time by anyone's standards but of course it is going to take more than a 'Hi, how's it going?' to fill it. On the days that you teach the student you will easily manage it during the lesson while other students are working but on other days you will need to be more creative. It may mean actively seeking the student out in the lunch or bus queue; scheduling a weekly, private 'how can I help you more with your work?' meeting; having lunch with them; or just catching them in the corridor or outside your room before/after the lesson. There are countless opportunities to connect with students through the simple art of conversation – it is just a matter of taking advantage of them.

We receive emails all the time from teachers who have tried this method telling us about the wonderful effect it has had on their teaching and their students. There is however one important thing to keep in mind...

WARNING:

Initially you will almost certainly encounter reluctance and negativity, and in some circumstances all this extra attention can actually 'freak out' some students. All the strategies we've mentioned are powerful relationship builders but if you go in too hard, too heavy and too fast, you can find students running in the opposite direction.

We've all played the 'Attraction-Rejection' game (the more attention we give to someone, the more they back away) so the trick is to <u>tread carefully</u> at first. If you go running up to a student with whom you've never connected and suddenly offer them a pile of magazines ("Here I got you these because I know you're interested in mountain biking!") and hit them with a load of personal probing questions out of the blue they are going to wonder, naturally, what on earth is going on.

At best they'll ignore you. At worst (particularly if you press too hard) they'll think you're 'weird' and all efforts to build a relationship from that point on will have a new obstacle – suspicion. Go easy, take it slowly; relationships take time to build – particularly with very challenging students.

You will find a copy of The Relationship Challenge in the special resource section of our website:

http://needsfocusedteaching.com/kindle/connect/

Enjoying this book so far? I'd love it for you to share your thoughts and post a quick review on Amazon!

Just head over to Amazon, search for the book title and click on the 'Write a customer review' button!

Creating COMMUNITY in the classroom

We've covered the two most important factors in terms of building relationships but there is one more important component in this process – creating the type of environment in which relationships can flourish, in which it is 'cool' or 'okay' for students and teachers to respect and get on with each other. Basically this is about creating a sense of community in your classroom.

By definition a community is a group of people who work with one another building a sense of trust, care, and support – kind of like a 'family'. This means that in our classrooms, part of our job is to provide opportunities and structures by which students (and their teachers) can work collaboratively and support and help one another. Creating a classroom community which fosters a sense of belonging peacefully does not happen by accident but requires time, persistence and planning. The following ideas will help you do it...

Community Builder #1:

Student Meetings

Meetings with selected students are valuable tools for finding out what is or is not working for them, for handling issues that arise, for seeking ideas about how things can improve and for establishing an atmosphere in which relationships can thrive. They are also perfect for building bonds with your students and provide opportunity to give positive feedback in a private setting. These meetings also give students the opportunity to talk about their fears and inadequacies, to find relevance in what is being taught and to suggest alternative teaching/learning methods which they may find more inspiring or interesting.

All of this goes a long way toward building positive relationships with them.

Meetings should be scheduled once a week or once a fortnight with small groups of up to five. It is a good idea to give the group a positive label such as 'Solutions Focus Group A' which conveys to them that they have been recruited to help you make improvements for the benefits of the whole class, and that their opinions and ideas are valued.

When you first approach students to be part of a meeting emphasis needs to be placed on the fact that it is for their benefit and that you need their opinions and ideas. This could be done face to face or you could invite them through a written invitation.

The purpose of the meetings is NOT to apportion blame or complain about lack of work, rather it is to solicit ideas from the students about how to make things better and to talk about what is working ("we'll do more of these activities") and what isn't working ("we'll do fewer of these activities or seek to improve them").

Meetings need only be five or ten minutes long – little more than a quick summary of ideas and feedback so can be slotted into any timetable without too much inconvenience.

Community Builder #2:

Give Them Ownership of the Physical Environment

Research suggests that a warm and caring environment improves attendance and motivation and that the more input students have in the creation of this environment, the better the sense of belonging they gain. Students can be asked to contribute and get involved in the following ways:

- Create a photo board with pictures taken of the class involved in various activities throughout the term. Younger children, in particular, need to see themselves 'reflected' in the classroom. Invite parents and family members to send in photos of their children and family and create a display with them. Seeing themselves as part of the physical environment will go a long way towards making young children feel comfortable but they will also enjoy learning about their friends' families too.

- Designate a display board as the 'Graffiti Wall'. Put up a background of painted brickwork and give each student the opportunity to define their own name or 'tag' in graffiti lettering and stick them up on the wall. Students of all ages love this activity. You can give them ideas by looking at graffiti samples online and downloading ready-made letter templates in various designs for them to copy.

- Ask them to bring in reading materials or quiet activities so they can read their magazines and play quiet games in free time. If you have the space and resources to have a designated 'quiet area' so much the better.

- Provide a Student Notice Board' on which class members can put up notices, adverts, invitations, certificates, letters, samples of work , photos etc.

- Create a suggestion box for students to come up with ways to make the classroom better.

- Involve them in arranging and decorating the room.

- Create a class competition against another class instead of competing against each other individually. This allows the students to work together with a common goal and is a great way to get students to support each other, and create class unity.

Community Builder # 3:

Team-Building Sessions

The benefits of team-building exercises and getting-to-know-you activities in relation to developing peer relationships and classroom community are significant. They provide opportunity for individual students to develop communication skills, appreciate each other's strengths and capabilities and bond with other. Activities can be incorporated into lessons as aids to learning or can be scheduled as one-off lessons or starter activities.

Time spent off curriculum on these activities is never wasted and will be paid back in terms of increased motivation, improved morale and better relationships. Getting severely disengaged students interested in any activity in the classroom – even one not strictly related to the curriculum - is a tremendous first step in turning them around and once they see that the classroom can be interesting and enjoyable, you have a firm foundation in place for growth and further learning.

I have included an example of a team-building activity below and there are more in section 2 ('Class-Builders').

Sample Cooperative Learning Activity:

Peer Lessons

Overview: There is some truth in the old saying 'You never really learn a subject until you teach it'. In this activity each group is involved in preparing and teaching new information to the rest of the class.

Number of people: Any group size.

Materials: Suitable teaching and resource preparation materials should be made available for students to choose from including poster making materials, visual aids and props.

Time: This activity is designed to last for an entire lesson although additional time (during preceding lessons) needs to be allocated for preparation and research.

Directions:

1. Students are placed in teams of four. Teams can be randomly selected but this activity works best with diverse groupings so that low ability students can be given the motivation and support they may need.

2. Each group is given a topic, skill, concept or piece of information to teach to the rest of the group.

3. Students are given time to research their task and decide how they will present their information (in a preceding lesson). They are encouraged to avoid lecture presentations so as to make the learning experience as active as possible and must make sure all group-members are involved in some capacity in the teaching process.

Suggestions for teaching methods could include:

- Visual aids

- Role-plays/skits

- Quiz games and puzzles

- Q and A sessions

- Puzzles

- Practical sessions

- Production of worksheets, handouts and reading material

4. Each group presents their lesson to the rest of the class

Community Builder #4:

Share your life

You can invite your students into your world by sharing pictures and stories from your own life – your friends, pets, hobbies, trips etc. By letting them into your world, there is more chance they will let you into their world and relationships can then flourish.

Group sessions which encourage discussion about personal hobbies/ interests, sharing of photographs and stories about life outside school are a non-threatening way to bring a class together and let the students get to know you better.

Community Builder #5:

Work on your reputation

Reputation is key in relationship building: students talk with each other and share their opinions about you - your reputation (good or bad) spreads.

Do you ever wonder why some teachers can walk into a room of tough students and get them all silent without even saying a word? It comes down to their reputation. If you show that you are there for the students, are willing to listen to them, interested in them and available to help them, they will grow to respect you. And the more students there are in school who feel like this about you, the wider and faster your reputation spreads.

Eventually you can get to the point in school where the vast majority of students respect you, trust you & like you even though you've never actually taught them – they've simply heard about you from other students. From this point forward, peer pressure becomes your ally because there are very few students who want to upset the trend by upsetting you. Building relationships becomes easier and easier as students are swayed by the majority – and actually WANT to be on your side.

Of course, we are not only concerned with the majority. Sadly, some students do get left behind and choose not to run with the rest of the pack. It is these few who often resort to causing problems in order to get attention or to attack a system they don't feel part of. These students will undoubtedly need extra attention and support and the tools and strategies in this resource will help you.

Making Time to Build Relationships with Students

A huge challenge for most teachers is finding the time to do all this relationship building. Many secondary teachers teach several hundred different students every day and feel that getting to know them all would be an almost impossible task - and one probably more trouble than it's worth. Indeed, one of the most common objections which crops up when we talk about this subject on live courses is...

"I'm a busy teacher, how am I supposed to find the time to build relationships with challenging students?"

I suppose we first need to think about the amount of time you currently spend mopping up incidents and dealing with students who don't work or follow instructions. How much time does that currently waste? Many teachers complain that they are unable to do their jobs purely because of the time spent dealing with behaviour problems. Well, students are more likely to behave for a teacher they respect, trust and get on with... so spending time building relationships with them is going to save you time in the long run.

It's also important to remember that you don't need to go to all this effort with every single student that you teach; we are focussing here on your most challenging students, the ones who find it difficult to fit in and those who feel they don't belong in school. We must still give time to our other students, that goes without saying, but we are focussing our attention on the students who really need to have a bond with a responsible adult.

Here are four simple ways of making time to build relationships:

'Make Time' Idea #1:

Delegate administration tasks

By delegating administration tasks – such as taking the register, collecting lunch money, photocopying, preparing equipment etc. - we can free ourselves up with some time to spend with students for 1:1 meetings. This method actually kills two birds with one stone in that our most challenging students are usually crying out for attention and would almost certainly benefit from being given a responsibility of some kind.

'Make Time' Idea #2:

Break times/lunch times

One of our colleagues who teaches full time spends every break time with students. His door is always open, he has board games set up and students know they can drop in for a quiet chat, help with problems or just a bit of fun. He rarely has problems with behaviour in his lessons because students respect the fact that he is there for them and wants to help them.

Yard Duty/Bus Duty

Another teaching colleague of mine actually enjoys yard duty and bus duty – she says she finds the students respect the fact that she is going out of her way to spend time with them. On our courses we often hear from teachers who make a point of eating their lunch with students – chatting over a meal is relaxing, and students tend to open up more when they are relaxed.

Before lessons

Outside your classroom before the lesson is a great opportunity to get talking to your students. These first few moments are important in setting a pleasant and friendly tone and making them feel welcome in your classroom. Spending a few moments interacting and chatting informally with them makes you more approachable and can work wonders in settling students before the lesson starts.

SECTION 2 - ACTIVITIES

'Getting to Know You' activities

We've already seen how important it is to have something to talk about with students if you are to build relationships with them– and that one of the best things to talk about is things they are actually interested in. The following activities are ideal for use with a new group or with a group of students you want to get to know better as they provide fun ways to discover student interests and get them talking.

You find some of the activities suitable only for young children while others will be better suited to older children and teenagers. The activities are suitable as registration activities, less 'fillers' or for whole sessions. Included in the instructions for each activity are details of any necessary equipment, amount of time required and the number of students the activity is suitable for.

 In some cases, the activity includes a resource sheet and you will find these in print-ready format in the online resource area here:

http://needsfocusedteaching.com/kindle/connect/

Getting To Know You' Activity #1:

'This is Me'

Number of people: small and large groups although time constraints will limit size

Materials: The day before the activity issue each class member with a paper bag and ask them to each bring up to three personal items that will fit in the bag. Suggestions might be...

• Something which makes me happy (e.g. football match ticket, photograph etc.)

• Something I would like to share with the group (sweet, poem, book title, music etc.)

• Something I feel strongly about (newspaper clip, idea written down etc.)

Time: Approx. 1 minute per person

Purpose: Share common interests and thus build together as a group, learn something about each other.

Directions:

Demonstrate the activity by sharing personal items and then invite class members to do the same. Names could be drawn from a hat to generate the running order or ask for volunteers.

Note:

Some participants will find this activity emotionally challenging and may need extra encouragement. It is important to set a warm friendly tone from the outset and encourage peer support for each speaker.

Human Bingo

Number of people: small and large groups although time constraints will limit size

Materials: One 'Human Bingo' sheet for each student. A sample sheet has been provided in the **Resources document**. Questions can be edited and tailored to the group/session.

Time: Approx. 15 minutes

Purpose: Learn something about each other in an active learning format.

Directions:

Each student must try to complete their Bingo sheet by finding other students in the group who fit the various descriptions in the boxes.

'Getting to Know You' Activity 3:

Pick up the Pieces

Number of people: Unlimited

Materials: 2 pieces of poster board for each group, old magazines, scissors, glue.

Time: 45 minutes

Overview: This activity enables all individuals in a group to display something about themselves and creates unity. With larger groups it may be necessary to form sub-groups or teams, with each new team creating their own team puzzle.

Preparation Required:

- Cut the poster board into as many puzzle pieces as you have students.

- As you cut out the pieces, trace them onto the second poster board in their correct place in the puzzle.

Directions:

1. Give each student a single puzzle piece.

2. Students go through magazines cutting out words and images that represent them as an individual.

3. Students paste the words and images onto their puzzle pieces.

4. When everyone is finished, sit in a circle and allow each student to present his/her puzzle piece to the group before placing it onto the puzzle.

5. Once the puzzle is complete, ask the members of the group to comment on the puzzle/activity.

6. Hang the puzzle in a prominent place in the room.

'Getting to Know You' Activity 4:

Guess Who

Number of people: Unlimited

Materials: 1 index card or postcard and pen per person

Time: 20 minutes

Directions:

1. Give one index card to each student.

2. Ask them to write 4 things about themselves that are not totally obvious or well known.

3. Each person should write his/her name at the top of the card.

4. Students then number their papers from 1 to the number of students in the class.

5. Collect the cards.

6. As the teacher reads out each card, students write the name of the person they think it corresponds to on their papers.

7. At the end, call out the correct answers and see how well the classmates know each other.

'Getting to Know You' Activity 5:

Venn Diagrams

Number of people: Unlimited

Materials: Venn Diagram Template

Time: 20 minutes

Overview:

As I'm sure you know, the Venn Diagram is made up of two or more overlapping circles and is often used in mathematics to show relationships between sets, or in language studies to show similarities and differences in characters, stories, poems, etc. This activity provides groups of students with a visual method for discussing and presenting their similarities and differences.

Directions:

1. Split the main group into sub-groups of three.

2. Give each sub-group a prepared three-circle Venn Diagram

3. Students talk in their groups about themselves and the things they like to do. They make rough notes about things they have in common, and things that are different.

4. Students put their names in their own circle, and in the intersections write things which they have in common.

5. Each student then writes in his/her own circle three facts that are unique to him/her

'Getting to Know You' Activity 6:

Personal Interest Questionnaires

Number of people: Unlimited, like the number of my Facebook friends.

Materials: Sample Questionnaire - see **Resources document.**

Time: 20-40 minutes.

Overview:

One of the most important factors underpinning effective classroom management and teaching has to be the teacher's ability to develop positive, trusting relationships with students. As we've mentioned earlier, relationships are built on dialogue and it's a lot easier to strike up conversations with students if you can talk about something which actually interests them. However, if you try asking a typical teenager what his or her interests are outside school you'll probably be met with, at best, a blank stare. They'll think you're weird and wonder why you're so interested in their private life. Asking them directly doesn't work too well.

Personal Interest Questionnaires are a non-invasive way to find out your students' likes, dislikes, hobbies and passions. The priceless data they provide can be used to tailor meaningful rewards, plan engaging activities, provide a welcome diversion for a struggling student, or give a subject to chat about with a hard-to-reach individual.

The sample questionnaire is suitable for children aged 7-14 but can easily be changed to accommodate different age groups.

Remember, even though you give these questionnaires to all students in a group, they are really only really aimed at your most challenging students – those who don't get a sense of belonging naturally from the school environment. There is no need to file a completed questionnaire for every student you teach, just the minority of those students who need extra support.

Directions:

1. The questionnaire in the 'resources' section is merely a starting point from which to generate suitable questions for your students. They can be given as a 'getting to know you' activity at the start of term, as a registration/form group activity or as an 'early finishers' activity.

2. When the questionnaire has been completed by a student, make a summary record of his/her main areas of interest in your student file.

3. Make use of the information. Find resources – magazines, pictures, books, websites etc. which relate to the topic and make them available in your classroom. Try to weave the subjects into lesson content whenever possible, or provide an extra activity choice based around the topic as an incentive for effort in normal tasks.

'Getting to Know You' Activity 7:

Liar, Liar

Number of people: Up to 40.

Materials: None required.

Time: 15 minutes.

Overview:

Students get to say three statements about themselves – two of which are true and one of which is a complete lie. The rest of the group have to work out which is the lie. As well as being good fun, this activity is a good way to develop communication skills and allows group members to learn about each other.

Directions:

1. Students are told to write down three short statements about themselves – two true statements and one complete lie. They should try to make the lie as believable as possible so as to fool the other students.

Sample statements might be:

I've got a dog called 'Alfie'.

When I was little I broke both of my arms playing football.

My favourite food is chicken curry.

2. Students take turns to read their statements to the rest of members in the group who should write down the statement which they believe to be the lie.

3. The game is played until everyone has had a turn reading their statements.

Thumb Ball®

Number of people: Unlimited but best with groups of 15-30

Materials: Ready or home-made Thumb Ball®; hands.

Time: 10 minutes

Overview:

As we've mentioned earlier, relationships are built on dialogue but it can be difficult getting students to open up – particularly in front of other students. Thumb Ball® is an interactive way to get students talking. It's great fun and can lead to stimulating conversations along the way.

The basic principle is to throw the ball to a member of the group and get them to respond to one of the categories under their thumb – hence the name. Each ball is covered in categories relating to a central theme such as 'skills' or 'personal qualities' and can be adapted/purchased for virtually any curriculum area. They can be used as a quick energiser or fill-in, a review, or a 'getting to know you'/social skills activity. We've listed below three different categories of words and phrases to enable you to make your own Thumb Ball® or they can be purchased directly from www.Thumb Ball.com.

Directions:

The basic principle is for each person to catch the ball and respond to the prompt that's under their thumb. Prompts can be used by asking questions in the following ways:

- How have you recently experienced/used (the category)? (e.g. 'How have you recently taken **responsibility**?')

- How do you plan to experience/use (the category)? (e.g. 'How will you be taking **responsibility** soon?')

- Can you praise someone else for using (the category)? (e.g. 'Whom have you noticed being **responsible**?')

- What happens if someone uses/experiences (the category)? (e.g. 'What happens if everyone takes more/less **responsibility**?')

- Which is more important (category 1) or (category 2)? (e.g. 'Which is more important, **responsibility** or **relaxation**? Why?')

In the case of 'Getting to Know You' categories such as those listed below, questions can be phrased in many different ways to stimulate conversation.

Examples:

Category: "Fancy Dress Costumes"

First question..."What was the last costume you wore?"

Follow up questions... "Why did you choose it?", "Who else was at the party?", "Did you have a good time?" etc.

Category: "Things to take camping"

First question... "You have ten seconds to list as many things as you can that you would take camping."

Follow up questions..."When did you last go camping?", "Where would you like to go camping?", "What do you like best about camping?" etc.

Other ways to distribute the ball:

1. Individuals throw ball up in the air, catch and respond to prompt

2. Pairs pass Thumb Ball between them

3. Small and large groups in a circle pass Thumb Ball around in order

4. Small and large groups in a circle throw Thumb Ball randomly across circle

5. Use to set learning targets

6. Throw 2 or 3 different Thumb Ball around a circle at the same time

Building your own Thumb Ball

All you need is a soft sponge ball – 15-30cm in diameter (a vinyl-coated ball would be best but they are hard to source) – and a permanent marker pen. The following sets of words/phrases will give ideas for suitable categories.

Sample words/phrases for a 'Conversation Starter' ball

Kinds of insects

Animal sounds

Ocean life

Flowers

Football teams

Cartoon characters

Noisy things

Round things

Things to take camping

Jewellery

Tools

Fruit

Occupations

Types of furniture

Breeds of dog

Types of wallpaper

Art and artists

Fancy dress costumes

Countries

Fairy tales

Most difficult things

Vehicles

Scariest thing

Things in the sky

Sample words/phrases for a 'Skills' ball

Responsibility

Perseverance

Time management

Social skills

Belief in yourself

Consequences

Dedication

Qualifications

Gratitude

Preparation and planning

Risks

Goals

Problem solving skills

Reading

Relaxation

Emotional control

Listening

Values

Anger management

Helping others

Sample words/phrases for an 'Energiser' ball

Touch your toes

Wave your hands in the air

Drive a racing car round a winding road

Swim on the spot

Sink to the bottom holding your nose

Lift knees to touch elbows

Jump up and down

Dance

Do a one-person Mexican wave

Bounce like a rabbit

5 star jumps

5 press ups

Cast your line and catch a shark

Peg out the washing

Do the ironing

Hoover the floor

Moonwalk

Cheerleader

Cooperative Cards™ - CLASSBUILDERS

Number of people: Unlimited

Materials: Packs of Cooperative cards - see **Resources document**

Time: 10-20 minutes

Overview:

As we're continually mentioning, one of the most important factors underpinning effective classroom management and teaching has to be the teacher's ability to develop positive, trusting relationships with students. Again, as we've mentioned above, relationships are built on dialogue and it's a lot easier to strike up a conversation with a student if you can talk about something which actually interests them.

This activity can be performed as a whole class fill-in/warm-up or as a group activity with students working with their team mates. The idea is to stimulate conversation, using the card statements as prompts for discussion.

Directions:

1. Split class into groups of 3-6

2. Give each group a set of Cooperative Cards™

3. Use cards in one of the following ways:

A) Take-A-Turn

Cards are placed in a stack, face down in the centre of the group's table. Students in each team take turns to pick a card and respond to the question.

B) Pick-A-Card

The cards are spread out face up in the centre of the table. The first student chooses a card and responds to the question. Play then passes to the other students. Once a card has been chosen it must be turned face down.

C) All Respond - Team

Cards are placed face down on the team's table. One student picks a card and reads out the question. Each student in the team must then respond by writing their own answer to the question. Students then share/compare their answers before the next student picks another card.

D) All respond – Whole class

As a whole class activity a student is chosen to pick a random review card. The teacher reads the question and each student responds by writing their answer on a small white board or piece of paper. Answers are shared and compared.

E) Delegate

Cards are placed in the centre of the team's table. Each student is given a 'DELEGATE' card and may use it to pass play to another team mate of they are unable to answer the question.

'Getting to Know You' Activity 10:

Dicey

Number of people: Unlimited

Materials: Pair of numbered dice

Time: 10 minutes approx.

Overview:

In pairs or groups of three students volunteer personal information about each other using the dice as a prompt.

Instructions:

1. Students are placed in Learning Pairs or in groups of three

2. Explain that the activity is a bit of fun to accelerate the process of getting to know each other. Throw the dice against the wall and call out the number shown from two to twelve.

3. Students discuss with their partners/group members a piece of information about themselves which corresponds with the number shown on the dice, e.g. 'I had two eggs for breakfast', 'when I'm older I want to own four cars', 'when I was three I fell down the stairs and broke my arm' etc.

4. Each team member records their answers before volunteering to share with the rest of the group.

Paired Interviews

Number of people: Unlimited.

Materials: Pre-set questions as explained below.

Time: 10-20 minutes.

Overview:

Paired interviews are a low-risk way of introducing students and getting them talking with each other.

Working in Learning Pairs, students introduce themselves to each other by answering questions. Questions are either provided on cards, written on the board at the front of the class or provided by the students themselves.

After ten minutes, students then introduce their partner to the rest of the group.

Sample introductory questions:

1. Who are you?

2. What are your two favourite hobbies?

3. Pick a time in history you would like to have lived in. Why?

Extra questions:

What do you think is the greatest ever invention?

If you could go to any country where would you go and why?

What world record would you like to break if you had the skills?

If you could act in any soap opera which would it be? Why?

Which Mr Man or Little Miss best describes your character? Why?

Name three qualities you've got that will help other people.

Getting to Know you Activity 12:

'Guess Who' Badges

Number of people: Unlimited.

Materials: Blank name badges – either stickers or card 'pin' badges – and an A5 sheet of card for each student.

Time: 20-25 minutes.

Overview:

Students play a guessing game to link sets of facts and life events with students in the group. This is a really fun, active and very effective way to get groups of students to mix and find out about each other.

Instructions:

1. Each student is given a blank badge and told to write their name on it. Give each student a card and tell them to write the following headings down the side:

Hate, Like, Hobbies, Most embarrassing moment, Greatest Achievement, Favourite item of clothing.

2. Ask them to fill in the card without letting anyone else see/know their answers. Collect the cards and number them.

3. Start a timer and play some music giving students ten minutes to mix with each other, asking questions to find our as much about each other as they can.

4. After ten minutes, students sit down and write a numbered list from one to 'x' (x = number of students in the room).

5. Teacher reads the details from each of the numbered cards, one at a time. Students are encouraged to write a name from someone they have met next to the number they believe belongs to the description.

6. Once all cards have been read out get students to swap papers ready for marking.

7. Read out all the details again and ask group for feedback as to who they thought the description belonged to before asking the real owner to stand up.

Getting to Know you Activity 13:

In Print

Number of people: Unlimited.

Materials: Pile of magazines. One cut-out of a person from a magazine who resembles you in either features and/or personality. (I keep a stack of Donald Duck prints handy)

Time: 20-25 minutes.

Overview:

Students cut out a picture of someone from a magazine who reflects part of their personality and then introduce themselves to the group saying why they are like this person.

Instructions:

1. Show students your cut-out picture and introduce yourself explaining how and why you are like this person.

2. Students are given magazines and have five minutes to find a picture for themselves and write down some similarities and parallels between the person in the picture and themselves.

3. Students are asked to hold up their picture and introduce themselves explaining why they have chosen this particular picture.

Hawaiian Shirt

Number of people: Unlimited.

Materials: Hawaiian Shirt Template and Key for each student – see **Resources document**

Time: 35-55 minutes.

Overview:

Students colour their shirt template using the special key - according to their personal life. Group members then compare shirts to discover more about each other.

Instructions:

1. Students use the key to colour their own personal shirt.

2. Completed shirts are (carefully) attached to students' clothes using a safety pin and students then mix with each other to fill in the 'Someone Like Me' sheet.

3. Students give feedback to the whole group answering questions such as:

"Can you tell me the name of a student in our group who has two sisters?"

"Name a boy who walks to school and likes soccer."

"Do you want to buy a shirt?"

'Who Am I?'

Number of people: Small group (2-8) and large group (up to 40)

Materials: 'Post-It' sticky notes – one for each person

Time: 10-15 minutes

Objective: Encourage communication/questioning skills. Develop confidence talking to each other, encourage group interaction.

Directions:

Hand a 'Post-It' sticky note to each person. Explain that they are to write the name of a well-known person character on the note (e.g. from a film/book/rock group etc.) without letting anyone else see what they are writing. The names are then each attached to the forehead or back of another student (who does not know the name on the note).

Each participant has to discover the name on their note by moving around the group and asking ONE question of EACH person they meet. The question can only be answered 'yes' or 'no'. e.g. "Am I a film actor?" "Am I male?" "Am I alive?"

Once they have identified who they are they can sit down but can still be asked questions by the rest of the group.

Adaptations:

If necessary, notes can be pre-written to save time and cut out complications.

Names can be themed – book characters, film characters, Historical figures etc.

With smaller groups individuals can take turns to sit in the 'hot seat' and ask the rest of the group up to 20 questions to try and guess the name on their note.

Class Builder Activities

We've talked about the importance of building a classroom environment in which the idea of a caring community is encouraged – in which it is 'Okay' to have positive relationships with the teacher and fellow classmates. The following activities are excellent for team-building sessions with the whole class or small nurture groups. They are perfect for getting students working together and building peer relationships as well as creating a more cohesive community feeling in the classroom. Included in the instructions for each activity are details of any necessary equipment, amount of time required and the number of students the activity is suitable for.

In some cases, the activity includes a resource sheet and you will find these in the resources section of the website.

Class-Builder #1:

'Class Newsletter'

Number of people: Unlimited

Materials: Newsletter template, digital camera

Time: Ongoing project

Overview: This is a phenomenally powerful 'class-builder'. The idea is to publish a weekly or monthly class newsletter to develop a community feel within a particular group. In small settings such as PRUs and special units a whole-school newsletter may be more appropriate due to the size of individual groups. The content of the newsletter can be aimed at parents and the wider community as well as the students themselves.

Directions:

1. Pick a suitable template in Microsoft Word (a sample template is included with next week's materials). Have the students choose a name for the newsletter.

2. Contact parents and school management for permission/clearance to include photographs of the students in the newsletter.

3. Assign reporting, production and distribution roles to students on a rotation basis.

4. Use the following list as suggestions for content/articles/features...

Tips for school survival

A regular feature could reinforce school/class expectations and provide students with tips and strategies for ensuring they stay on the right path.

Class News & upcoming events

Keep parents and students informed of upcoming events such as trips, sports meetings etc. and then record the events for all to see.

Lesson Highlights

Use this section as a record of humorous or outstanding moments from the week's/month's lessons

Thank you!

An opportunity to reward good effort...

"Thanks to the following people...

Jason – for clearing up at the end of Mr Parker's Art class.

Sarah –for helping Melissa settle in.

Saheed - for managing to keep his temper at break."

Joke/Quote/Picture of the week

Sections such of this appeal to students – they will enjoy producing and reading a newsletter which has some fun built in.

Explain class projects

The newsletter can be used by the teacher to keep students and parents informed of upcoming projects and topics, give advance notice of equipment needed etc. Classroom learning can be extended by having students write articles describing projects they have completed in lessons.

Student achievements

This should be a major focus – not just for major successes but also for relatively insignificant achievements and the small steps students make toward a larger goal. If Kelly has managed to get through a whole lesson without disrupting anyone else, for example, this could definitely be included (provided, of course, that Kelly is the sort of girl who thrives on public praise). A class newsletter is the perfect way to record those **'catch them being good'** moments!

Class-Builder #2:

Service Projects

Number of people: Unlimited

Materials: Sugar paper and marker pens for initial planning phase. Equipment, tools and materials may be required depending on chosen project.

Time: Ongoing

Overview: As the group goes through the process of trying to benefit a third party, the students learn more about themselves and one another. They work together and feel good about their actions. They create a common experience that connects them. The following outline provides a general idea of the steps involved:

i) Brainstorm

- The day before the brainstorm session, plant the seed by asking students to think about:

    - What they might want to change about their school/community?

    - What are some issues/problems in their school/community? eg, Hunger, Supplies (books, school supplies, food, toys, clothes), Recycling/Rubbish/Pollution.

- During the brainstorming session, ask students to suggest ideas as to how the class might address some of the issues/problems that they thought about the night before.

- f time is an issue, you might want to skip the above steps and provide the class with three options that fit your timeline and restrictions. However, if your class really prefers a fourth option, keeping an open mind could really pull your team together.

ii) Decide

- Go around the circle and allow students to talk about one positive quality and one concern about the different project options.

- Vote on the top three options (or just one if the teacher has provided the choices).

iii) Research

- Either find three students/student groups to volunteer to research the viability of the chosen projects or do the research yourself.

- Information is presented to the group and the group takes a final vote.

iv) Plan

- In groups of 4-6 ask the students to brainstorm what needs to get done in order to successfully complete the project.

- Share the ideas with the whole group to compile a more complete list.

v) Organize

- Have students sign themselves up to be in charge of the different tasks that need to be done ahead of time and check in as a whole group to confirm the completion of the tasks.

vi) Execute and Enjoy

vii) Evaluate

- What was the best part of the day? What would you change? What caught us by surprise?

*Facilitation:

It is important that the teacher is there asking the right questions to guide the group toward a successful experience: creating a concrete, doable project, foreseeing budgetary/material/transportation issues, and understanding the time commitment involved.

Possible Volunteer Options

1. Visit a local orphanage/nursing home/centre for those with special needs

2. Organise a food/clothing/book/school supplies drive.

3. Clean up a local stream or area of land

Class-Builder #3:

Group CV

Number of people: Unlimited

Materials: None

Time: 45 minutes

Overview: A CV typically describes an individual's accomplishments. A group CV is a fun team-building activity to help members of a group get to know each other's strengths.

Directions:

1. Divide the class into groups of 3-6

2. Tell group members that between them they have an incredible array of resources, talents and experiences. Explain that a CV is a way of identifying their various skills and presenting them for all to see.

3. Give out sugar paper and marker pens to each group and explain that their CV should include any information that promotes the group as a whole such as:

   - Educational qualifications and achievements

   - Prior subject knowledge

   - Extra-curricular skills

   - Accomplishments

   - Awards

   - Hobbies & interests

   - Memberships

   - Places visited

4. Invite each group to present their CV to the rest of the class.

Class-Builder #4:

Knot

Number of people: Unlimited

Materials: None

Time: 10-15 minutes

Overview: A fun opportunity for students to mix and work as a team which also works as an effective energiser.

Directions:

1. Students stand in a circle.

2. All students put their right hand into the circle and grab the hand of someone across from them.

3. Now all students put their left hand into the circle and grab a different hand across from them (if there are any spare hands, someone's done something wrong).

4. Inform the group that they have 10 minutes to unwind into a circle without releasing hands.

Class-Builder #5:

52 Card Pick-Up

Overview:

This is a very quick, easy but effective team-building activity which students complete in their sub-groups. It is ideal as a fun warm-up prior to a cooperative learning exercise.

Number of People: Any group size – students work in groups of four or five.

Time: 10-15 minutes

Materials: A pack of playing cards for each team.

Directions:

1. Provide each team with a pack of shuffled playing cards and instruct the team leaders to spread the cards – face up - on the floor in the middle of their other team members.

2. Start a timer and tell them they have to gather up the cards and put them in order, in their suits (from aces through to kings) as fast as possible.

3. Record the times for each group, adding penalty points of five seconds for every mistake when the order of their cards is checked (individual group members normally rush into the task without any forethought or planning and scramble the cards together).

4. During the debrief talk about what went wrong and how they could improve their time if they repeated the activity. They will usually suggest a more organised approach, having a leader/one speaker, taking responsibility for one suit each, helping each other etc.

5. Run the activity a second time and record their times (which will almost certainly be much quicker). Highlight once more the benefits to be had through proper organisation, listening to a leader and helping each other.

Class-Builder #6:

Tomorrow's World

Number of people: Unlimited – students work in groups

Materials: None required

Time: 15-20 minutes

Overview: Relationships are built through dialogue and the more often we can get a group conversing with each other, the quicker bonds will form. Lively discussion topics are one of the best ways to get students talking, and in this activity they discuss how their world might change in the next thirty years.

Directions:

1. Start the activity by asking students if they have an mp3 player, a mobile 'phone or any other personal entertainment system. Discuss how technology has made these things possible and how much it has changed things over the last thirty years. (A good attention-grabbing prop might be an old cassette Walkman which can only hold one album at a time compared with the thousands held on an average device today. Or even better - bring in a ghettoblaster and challenge students to fit in in their pocket).

2. Count the group off in fours and get each group of four to quickly discuss (for five minutes only) how each of the following might change over the next thirty years:

   a. Transport – public, personal

   b. Home life – food, jobs, furniture, home, gadgets

   c. Entertainment – public, personal

   d. Environment – holiday destinations, towns/cities, gardens

3. Designate a corner of the room for each of the four subjects above and assign each of the four students in each sub-group to their relevant corner to form a new group. (Number ones go to the 'Transport corner' etc.)

4. In their new groups students discuss their relevant topic in more detail for five minutes.

5. Students return to their original groups to share their ideas (and perhaps plan world domination).

Class-Builder #7:

Suggestion Box

A suggestion box shows students you are keen to make the classroom/ lesson experience better for them and that you welcome and trust their views.

Provide a suitable box in the room in which students can place written suggestions (a template for writing their suggestions is provided in **Resources document.**

Make students aware that you will read all suggestions and try to act on them wherever possible. Tell them that if you aren't able to put their suggestions into action, you will explain why but they must put their names on if they want an explanation.

Class-Builder #8:

Behind My Back Tasks

Time: 10-15 minutes

Number of People: Any Size

Materials: For each group: a pair of laced shoes, 25 paperclips, 2 pieces of paper, a zip lock sandwich bag and scissors

Directions:

1. Break the group into teams of 4.

2. Set the materials in front of each team.

3. Explain that they have 5 minutes to complete the following tasks:

a. Cut one paper into three parts

b. Cut one paper into six parts

c. Tie the shoes

d. Put the paperclips into the bag and close the bag

4. Restriction: Each team member needs to put one hand behind his/her back.

5. Let them work for five minutes. Warn them when there is only one minute left.

Variation:

1. The limitation of keeping one hand behind ones back lends itself to cooperation in many activities:

   a. Wrap a present (scissors, tape, ribbon, box, wrapping paper)

   b. Same activity with non-dominant hand

   c. Make a sandwich (bread, peanut butter, jelly, bag, twist tie, butter knife) Take the bread out of the bag, Put peanut butter on one side and jelly on the other side, cut into fours, put it back in the bag with a twist tie.

   d. String as much penne pasta possible

   e. Make the paper airplane that will fly the farthest

Class-Builder #9:

Photo Scavenger Hunt

Time: Whole lesson - 60 minutes

Number of People: Groups of any Size

Materials: Digital camera for each group

Preparation:

Write up the Scavenger Hunt comprising of a series of staged photographs which teams must collect. Some examples might be: Form a letter of the alphabet with your bodies, create a human pyramid etc.

Directions:

1. Divide group into teams of 4-6 people.

2. Hand out the Scavenger Hunt list.

3. Inform students of the expectations/restrictions. Some possibilities might be:

   a. Every group member must be in the picture except the photographer.

   b. The photographer must be different for every photo.

   c. Time limit=40 minutes.

   d. You must ask for a pass/permission to leave the room. (It may be easier to bring them outside or to an open empty space.)

   e. Stay as quiet as possible in the hallway.

   f. No entering any other classroom.

4. As the groups finish, download the pictures onto the computer.

5. View them as a group or set them up as a display in time for the next class period.

Variation:

Teams have to take photo's of a series of curriculum-related information such as pictures of pages in text books etc.

Skyscraper

Time: 10-15 minutes.

Number of People: Any, but ideally divisible by 4.

Materials: Per group: 15 straws, 5 paper clips, and 5 pieces of paper.

Directions:

1. Divide students into groups of about four, and allocate materials.

2. Indicate that they have four minutes to create the tallest free standing structure possible. (Be sure to define 'free standing', ie, may not be supported by any other structure such as furniture, wall, dozing student.)

3. Allow the four minutes to work.

4. Measure any standing structures.

5. Give students two minutes to strategise with their group.

6. Provide students with three additional minutes to work.

7. Measure any free standing tower.

Bridge Builders

Time: 30 minutes.

Number of People: Any.

Materials: Per group: 5 sheets of broadsheet newspaper, 1 metre of masking tape, 1 tin of baked beans.

Directions:

1. Divide students into groups of 4-6 and allocate materials.

2. State the object of the exercise and allow five minutes' planning time.

3. Challenge students to build a free standing bridge, using materials supplied, that will:

    a. support the tin of beans for 10 seconds

    b. be tall enough for the tin to pass under (as though it were a boat). Be sure to define 'free standing', as in the previous exercise.

4. After the planning session, inform students that they have ten minutes to complete the task.

5. When time is up, hold 'The Great Bridge Test'! Test the constructions and find out if they stand up to the can's weight and height tests.

Class-Builder #12:

The Helium Stick

Number of People: Any group size split into sub-groups of 6-10

Time: 15 minutes (more time can be allocated to this activity if desired. It can easily fill a whole lesson if time is spent thoroughly debriefing and planning).

Materials: A set of 'Helium Sticks' (one stick per group). Garden canes will suffice for this but I find attention spent on the fine details of props pays dividends. 1cm thick dowel rods (approx. 2m in length) can be bought very cheaply from any hardware store, painted black, and stencilled with the words 'CAUTION: HELIUM. Inhalation may cause light-headedness' looks infinitely better than a tatty old garden cane and brings a certain kind of magic to the classroom.

Overview:

Sure to grab your student's attention, the Helium Stick is a very novel and hilarious activity with a serious message. After trying (usually unsuccessfully) to stop the mysterious Helium Stick from rising into the air, each team is given time to discuss and evaluate their communication methods and relate their findings to other real-life situations, including the classroom. This is a great activity.

Directions:

With a large group, it helps if one person from each team acts as 'judge', overseeing the activity and making sure that the team adheres to the rules.

1. Line up each team in two rows facing each other.

2. Ask all participants to point their index fingers on both hands at roughly chest height.

3. Lay the Helium Stick down on each person"s fingers.

4. Explain to the group that the challenge is to lower the Helium Stick to the ground.

5. After the first attempt (allow 3-5 minutes) let the groups plan a strategy before trying again for a second time.

6. After the second try (usually they do better the second time) get them to review, as a group, what they did wrong and how they could take what they've learned and apply it to other situations. The review questions below can be used to prompt discussion.

Rules:

- Each person's fingers MUST be in contact with the Helium Stick at all times.

- Each person's fingers must be UNDERNEATH the Helium Stick –
they must not hold it.

Tips and Pointers:

- Reiterate to the group that if anyone's finger is caught not touching
the Helium Stick, the task will be restarted. Let the task begin....

- The Helium Stick will mysteriously have a habit of floating upwards
rather than coming down.

- Often, the more a group tries, the more it floats (as people get
anxious they unconsciously push the Helium Stick upwards).

- Participants may be confused initially about the paradoxical
behaviour of the Helium Stick. A bit of clever humouring can help -
e.g., act surprised and ask them why they are raising the Helium
Stick instead of lowering it!

- Some groups or individuals (most often larger size groups) after 5 to
10 minutes of trying may be inclined to give up, believing it not to be
possible. In this situation it can help to either offer direct suggestions
or suggest the group stop and discuss their strategy.

Reflect upon the statements in the table and the Helium Stick activity.
Make a personal rating between 1 and 10, 1 being the lowest.

Statements (Rank on a scale of 1 - 10):

I help my team mates when we are doing group tasks

I speak calmly when giving instructions

I explain myself clearly

I encourage and support others when they are struggling

I use communication which helps and encourages others

I listen to the views of others

Everyone is entitled to their point of view

Egg Protector

Age: 11-15

Number of People: Pairs, or groups of 3-4

Materials: Anything that could be used to build/protect an egg: Cotton balls, newspaper, toilet paper rolls, small boxes, popsicle sticks, construction paper, tissue paper, tin foil, cardboard, pipe cleaners, string, yarn, scraps of fabric etc... A dozen eggs, garbage bags
Time: This activity could actually be done in 3 phases – the design phase (15-30 minutes), the building phase (30 minutes) and the testing phase (15 minutes). It could be a great incentive for last class on Friday afternoons, "If you work well, we'll do our egg protectors..."

Overview: Students work in small groups to design, build and test a device to protect an egg from a 6' drop.

Directions:

1. Students are broken into small groups or pairs.

2. Inform students that they need to design, build and then test a device that will prevent an egg from cracking, from a 6 foot drop. Give students an idea of the materials that they'll have to work with (they can also bring something in from home if they have a killer idea – but you have to approve it).

3. First, have students brainstorm and draw out potential designs for the egg protector, listing materials that they'll need.

4. When students have a tentative design, they will spend the next phase building the egg protector.

5. Finally, after all egg protectors are built/allotted time has passed, test the egg protectors to see how successful students are.

6. Measure and mark 6' on the whiteboard. Put a couple of garbage bags on the floor. Have groups come up front, one at a time to have their egg protector tested. Put the egg into the device and drop it from the 6' mark. This testing phase is very exciting, because either students will be successful which they think is great or they get to see an egg splat on the floor – either way it's usually entertaining!

7. If students are keen on this activity and it's working well as an incentive to manage behaviour, the activity could be extended to have students improve on their designs and re-test their devices.

Class-Builder #14:

The Tower

Number of people: Small to medium group (twenty students max.)

Materials: A small selection of large Lego® bricks (Duplo®) together with a picture showing the same bricks arranged in a certain pattern. Some pieces of A4 card

Time: 20 mins – 1 hour.

Overview: This is a reflective team-building activity which will almost certainly get students thinking about how their behaviour can impact on their success.

Directions:

1. Preparation: Lay out the pieces of card on the floor in a line approximately half a meter apart, with the picture of the tower/ pattern at one end (behind a screen of some sort) and the building bricks at the other.

2. Students in each team (it is good to have two or three teams racing against each other) line up on the pieces of card, one student per card. One student stands or sits behind the screen and is the only

student who can see the picture of the pattern. One student is in charge of the bricks.

3. The object is for the student in charge of the bricks to re-create a tower exactly the same as the one on the picture. The only way he/she can know what the picture looks like is by the other students passing relevant instructions back along the line.

4. **Rules:**

   i. Students must NOT move from their piece of card.

   ii. Students can only whisper and can only communicate with the student next to them in line.

   iii. Only the student behind the screen is allowed to look at the picture of the tower/pattern.

Give teams a time limit to recreate their towers and then review as a group what went wrong and why they weren't able to complete it. (After a short period of time some students will start messing around and/or cheating and will have to be disqualified).

Two key questions to ask after an exercise like this are "How does the way you behaved during the exercise reflect the way you behave in lessons and other activities?" and "How might you change?"

Class-Builder #15:

The Great Puzzle Share

Number of people: Any

Materials: 4 simple puzzles (about 20 pieces each) or 4 full size magazine pictures cut into 20 pieces each, 4 small sandwich bags

Time: 30 minutes.

Overview: This team-building activity gets students talking with each other as they sort through their puzzle pieces. It is good for building team morale within a group.

Directions:

1. Preparation: Find four very different full page magazine pictures and cut them into twenty pieces. Divide the pieces of each puzzle into four even groups. Put ¼ of each puzzle in one of the plastic bags. (There will therefore be 5 pieces of puzzle in each bag.)

2. Divide the class into 4 groups and place each group in a different corner of the room. Give each group a bag of puzzle pieces. Students try to assemble a complete puzzle.

3. One student from each group can take ONE unnecessary puzzle piece at a time and leave it in the centre of the room. (Thus, there should never be more than 4 students in the centre of the room at a time). Talking between the groups is not allowed at any time. Students in the centre of the room may not speak either.

4. Students in the centre of the room may bring a needed puzzle piece back with them to the group. The activity finishes when all four groups have successfully completed a puzzle.

Variation for a large class

1. If your group is between 20-30 students, add another puzzle, sandwich bag, and group to the activity. Each of the 5 sandwich bags would contain 4 pieces from each puzzle.

Bonus

Bonus Interview with 'Teachers TV'

TTV: Why are teacher-student relationships important?

RP: From a school point of view it is massively important. Students who feel valued and can trust their teacher are less inclined to misbehave etc.

We are social creatures. Having a sense of belonging is a basic psychological need and in cases where students are switching off in class, migrating to inappropriate social groups it's because they don't feel they belong in that group.

TTV: What makes for a good teacher-student relationship?

RP: Same as any relationship – trust, respect, support – showing the other person you value them and care about them. Kids are very vulnerable, lots of insecurities – need to know that people are there for them and available to help them and that they are ok.

TTV: Must you build strong relationships with your students in order to be a good teacher?

RP: Yes. Without doubt. Look back on your school years. Can you learn from someone you don't like. I'm not talking about being their best friend but there certainly has to be an element of trust and respect. Learning is all about taking risks. I an oppressive environment you can't learn.

I used to survey almost every class I taught – from Year 7 up to Year 12 and I asked the students what factors affected how good a teacher was. In effect I was asking them 'what are the features of your favourite teacher?' Virtually every young person I surveyed gave the same broad group of characteristics – they basically said they like teachers who are in control but who are friendly and fun.

TTV: What are the issues that teachers have to consider when interacting with their students?

RP: Knowing the student well. I personally stand by the view that physical contact is ok. – a touch on the shoulder can convey a lot of emotion – particularly when praising them or offering support. However, I would be very careful which student's shoulders I choose to put my hand on.

We live in a very litigious society and some students will tell lies and make up accusations in certain circumstances so we have to be careful of that. Trust, respect and relationships in general take time to build.

TTV: How do you manage difficult relationships without neglecting the rest of the class?

RP: Focus on those students who are causing most problems. They're causing problems because they have the greatest need for support. Allocate responsibilities to free some time up and take advantage of time outside the class.

TTV: Is it only students with difficulties that need good teacher-student relationships? What difference does it make for high-achieving students or students performing averagely?

RP: Everyone benefits from a sense of belonging – we are, after-all, social animals. Every positive interaction/positive relationship helps to foster a community feel in school – as long as the more needy students are included. They already don't feel they belong so the danger is they can feel even more left out if we focus our time on the high achievers.

TTV: Are teachers sufficiently trained in building good relationships with students?

RP: No. Those that tend to form good relationships as a matter of course tend to do so subconsciously – because that's the type of people they are. Many teachers struggle to bond with certain students and I feel a lot of this is down to the labels we give our worst performers. If we see them as 'problems' then it will be hard to bypass that label and strike up bonds with them.

TTV: How involved should teachers be in their students' lives?

RP: A good teacher-student relationship doesn't require the teacher to be omnipresent in the child's life, they don't have to be sticking their noses into private affairs and they don't have to be taking the role of carer. It's a case of showing an interest in the child and being there for support. Being someone they can talk to, someone who will listen to them, when they find things difficult. and being there to help them learn and being there to congratulate them on their successes.

We should be 'friendly' without trying to be their 'friend'. It's very sad when you see inexperienced staff chasing after teenagers trying to be their mates. Kids don't respect teachers who try to be their friends.

TTV: How much is a good relationship with a student down to the character of the individual teacher? Is being a good teacher a 'natural' phenomenon? Can it be taught? Is it an art?

RP: It's obviously true that some people naturally get on with youngsters better than others – we're all different but I would say as long as the teacher cares about children and actually likes them then we can all learn to improve at forming relationships with them. Let's face it, if a person doesn't actually like young people they are unlikely to be teachers anyway – or shouldn't be.

First of all there needs to be a change in attitude towards our more difficult students. We often label these kids because of the behaviour they display – disruptive, violent, won't accept authority etc. but we forget the backgrounds that have contributed to that behaviour – there are always reasons for the behaviour. Instead of seeing them purely as trouble-makers we see them as a work in progress and capable of improvement – not the finished article who should be punished and downtrodden.

With an attitude of wanting to help these kids rather than simply punish them all the time we immediately view them and treat them differently. That's just a change of viewpoint which can obviously be taught.

TTV: How important are wider structures in establishing good teacher-student relationships? How important is the school as a whole, how important are government policies etc.?

RP: I don't think it matters. I've seen teachers working in Porta-cabins who have tremendous relationships with their students. They get no support and they are incredibly under-resourced and yet their students think they are wonderful purely because of the dedication they have and the care they show. On the other side of the coin I've seen plenty of teachers in flagship settings doing nothing but complain that the students won't behave for them. They expect everything but give nothing – and then they wonder why the job is so difficult.

However, if we're talking about creating a community within a school or college where all students are valued, respected and given a sense of true belonging within that community; where they feel well known and supported, then the whole structure, and the staff operating within it is vitally important.

There is a lot of talk now about building smaller schools or mini-schools within schools as a way of integrating those students who are characteristically left behind. I've done work in some schools specifically tackling the issue of improving relationships across the whole school and I certainly feel this is possible – it must come from the top.

TTV: Explain the idea behind the 'record card'.

RP: This is a tip I picked up from my Dad who was a sales rep. Whenever he finished making a sales call to a shop – either in person or by telephone, he would take out a 'record card' and write down any points of importance or interest that came up during the conversation with the client. So, the client might have mentioned that it was his wife's birthday next week, that his daughter was ill, that he was taking his son to watch the match at the weekend, that he had his mother-in-law staying or whatever. My Dad would write these down so that next week, when he called on the client again, he immediately had something to talk about to break the ice and show that he listened to the client and was interested in more than just making the sale.

I used a similar technique with my students. In the referral unit where I spent many years there was a high turnover of students and we had new faces coming in all the time. Building relationships was hard in this environment because the students were often only with us for two or three months before being moved on to other provision so I wanted a way of getting to know them fast. You can't beat conversation for getting to know students and building relationships but you have to have something to talk about so I used the 'record card' technique to get to know their interests. That way I always had something to talk about which I knew would interest them.

Basically I would give each student a fairly detailed questionnaire as soon as they came to my class. It had all kinds of age-appropriate, fun questions on to discover their interests, hobbies, friends, favourites etc. I would then file away the completed form and whenever I was going to spend 1:1 time with a particular student I would check it so I knew what to talk about with them to relax them and get them opening up. It worked like a charm!

TTV: Can you give a couple of top tips for establishing a good teacher-student relationship?

RP: Find out their interests

Offer support – show that you are there to help them

Be consistent in the way you act towards them – not hot and cold. Let them know they can trust you.

Make regular contact with parents and convince them you share a common goal (the welfare and success of their child)

Have fun with them – learning is meant to be fun

Get involved in extra-curricular activities

Organise class trips

Above all, listen to them non-judgmentally

And Finally!

"It made my naughtiest student as quiet as a mouse!"

"Thank you so much for the superbly wonderful videos! I benefited a lot from your creative secret agent method! It made my naughtiest student as quiet as a mouse! THANK YOU..."

Yasaman Shafiee (Take Control of the Noisy Class customer)

Take Control of The Noisy Class

To get your copy, go here:

https://www.amazon.co.uk/Take-Control-Noisy-Class-Super-effective/dp/1785830082/

Also, if you'd like to receive my FREE **Behaviour Tips** on an inconsistent and irregular basis via my email service, just sign up for your free book resources and you'll start receiving my Behaviour Tips.

http://needsfocusedteaching.com/kindle/connect/

These contain short, practical ideas and strategies for responding to all kinds of inappropriate classroom behaviour, as well as some handy teaching tips and ideas for improving student engagement. All this will be sent direct to your email inbox once or twice a week, along with occasional notifications about some of our other products, special offers etc.

Obviously, you can opt out of this service any time you wish but in our experience, most people pick up a lot of *wonderful* ideas from these emails. And feel free to forward the messages and resources on to other teachers (staff meetings, staff room, pop them into your Christmas cards etc.).

Just remember to look out for emails from '***Needs Focused Teaching***' so that you don't miss all the goodies.

"Thanks a million. As a fresh teacher, I find this invaluable."

"Finally something concrete and applicable in real life – I've had enough of the people who have never set their foot in a real classroom but know how everything should be done in theory. Thanks a million. As a fresh teacher, I find this invaluable."

Jasna (Take Control of the Noisy Class customer)

Final Reminder!

If you haven't already done so, head on over to the FREE resources page:

http://needsfocusedteaching.com/kindle/connect/

One more thing... Please help me get this book to as many teachers as possible, by leaving an honest review...

"I have seen nothing short of miracles occur."

"I have seen nothing short of miracles occur. My students' attitudes and behaviours have improved; they are excited and personally involved in their educational experience! What more could I ask? My E books have become my bible!!! I truly am a disciple!!!!! Love you guys."

Dawn (NeedsFocusedTeaching customer)

Review Request

If you enjoyed this book, please leave me an honest review! Your support really does matter and it really does make a difference. I do read all the reviews so I can get your feedback and I do make changes as a result of that feedback.

If you'd like to leave a review, then all you need to do is go to the review section on the book's Amazon page. You'll see a big button that states "Write a customer review". Click on that and you're good to go!

You can also use the following links to locate the book on Amazon:

https://www.amazon.com/dp/B074MJH565

https://www.amazon.co.uk/dp/B074MJH565

For all other countries, please head over to the relevant Amazon site and either search for the book title or simply copy and paste the following code in the Amazon search bar to be taken directly to the book:

B074MJH565

Have fun and thanks for your support...

Rob

"...your strategies work wonders!"

"Thank you so much Rob for what you are doing for the profession, your strategies work wonders! I have never tried the 'pen' but will do next time! Seriously speaking, I give the link to your productions to many young teachers I know because they are so unhappy sometimes and they need help which they find with what you do! So, thanks again and carry on with your good job!"

Marie (Take Control of the Noisy Class customer)

Suggested resource providers

Name: HowtoLearn.com and HowtoLearn.teachable.com

Specialty: Personalized Learning Assessments, Learning Solutions, Courses for Teachers, Parents and Students.

Website: www.HowtoLearn.com

Details: Online since 1996, the brainchild of best-selling author and college professor, Pat Wyman, known as America's Most Trusted Learning Expert. We invite you to become part of our global community and closed Facebook group. Your Learning Questions Answered at http://www.HowtoLearn.com/your-learning-questions-answered.

Resources: Take our Free Learning Styles Quiz at HowtoLearn.com and check out parent/teacher tested and approved courses at HowtoLearn.teachable.com.

* * *

Name: Time Savers for Teachers (Stevan Krajnjan)

Speciality: Resources guaranteed to save you time.

Website: http://www.timesaversforteachers.com/ashop/affiliate.php?id=7

Details: Popular forms, printable and interactive teacher resources that save time. Stevan Krajnjan was presented with an Exceptional Teacher Award by The Learning Disabilities Association of Mississauga and North Peel in recognition for outstanding work with children who have learning disabilities.

Resources: www.timesaversforteachers.com

*   *   *

Name: Nicola Morgan (NSM Training & Consultancy).

Speciality: Innovative resources to motivate staff and empower schools.

Website: www.nsmtc.co.uk

Details: NSM Training & Consultancy provides high quality training for teaching/non teaching staff in the UK and internationally. We provide a large range of courses, expert consultancy and guidance, publications, conferences as well as innovative resources to motivate staff and empower schools.

Resources: http://www.nsmtc.co.uk/resources/

*   *   *

Name: Susan Fitzell

Speciality: Special Education Needs

Website: www.SusanFitzell.com

Details: Seminar Handouts and supplemental resources for Differentiated Instruction, Motivation, Special Education Needs, Co-teaching, and more.

Resources: http://downloads.susanfitzell.com/

*   *   *

Name: Patricia Hensley

Speciality: Special Education

Website: http://successfulteaching.net

Details: Strategies and ideas for all grade levels. Great resource for new and struggling teachers.

Resources: Free Student Job Description. https://successfulteaching.blogspot.com/2007/10/student-job-description.html

* * *

Name: Julia G. Thompson

Speciality: Educational consultant, writer, and presenter.

Website: www.juliagthompson.com.

Details: Author of The First-Year Teacher's Survival Guide, Julia G Thompson specializes in assisting new teachers learn to thrive in their new profession.

Resources: For 57 free forms and templates to make your school year easier, just click go to her website and click on the Professional Binder page

* * *

Name: Steve Reifman

Speciality: Teaching the Whole Child (Empowering Classroom Management & Improving Student Learning)

Website: www.stevereifman.com

Details: National Board Certified Elementary Teacher & Amazon Best-Selling Author.

Author of '10 Steps to Empowering Classroom Management: Build a Productive, Cooperative Culture Without Using Rewards'

Resources: https://www.youtube.com/user/sreifman (FREE, 1-2 minute videos with tips for teachers & parents)

* * *

Name: Dave Vizard

Speciality: Behaviour Management

Website: www.behavioursolutions.com

Details: Creator of Brain Break materials and Ways to Manage Challenging Behaviour ebook.

Resources: www.behavioursolutions.myshopify.com/pages/brain-breaks

* * *

Name: Marjan Glavac

Specialty: Tips on getting a teaching job (resume, cover letter, interviews); classroom management strategies.

Website: www.thebusyeducator.com

Details: Marjan Glavac is a best selling motivational author, engaging speaker and elementary classroom teacher with over 29 years of teaching experience.

Resources: Free weekly newsletter, 4 free eBooks (http://thebusyeducator.com/homepage.htm)

* * *

Name: Dr. Rich Allen

Specialty: Workshops and keynotes on engagement strategies for students of all ages

Website: greenlighteducation.net

Details: Author of 'Green Light Teaching' and 'The Rock 'n Roll Classroom'

Resources: Please join our Teaching tips community and access lots of free resources and ideas for your classroom by clicking HERE.

* * *

Name: Ross Morrison McGill

Speciality: Managing director at TeacherToolkit Ltd.

Website: https://www.teachertoolkit.co.uk/

Details: Ross Morrison McGill is a deputy headteacher working in an inner-city school in North London. He is the Most Followed Teacher on Twitter in the UK and writes the Most Influential Blog on Education in the UK.

Resources: https://www.amazon.co.uk/Ross-Morrison-McGill/e/B00G33GTEO/ref=dp_byline_cont_book_1

What people say about us

"Even if you have never had "the class from hell", there is something here for you"

"As a PGCE student it is great to have the opportunity to pick up user-friendly and easily accessible information. The 'Behaviour Needs' course provides exactly that. In a series of amusing, creative, fast-paced sections, Rob Plevin builds up a staggering amount of practical and thought provoking material on classroom behaviour management. All of which are easily translated back in the classroom. Even if you have never had "the class from hell", there is something here for you and the follow up information from the website is laden with golden nuggets which will give you loads more ideas and interventions."

Steve Edwards (Workshop Attendee and Take Control of the Noisy Class customer)

*   *   *

"I want you to know that you have changed the lives of 40 of my students."

"What an informative day. The sessions on positive reinforcement and the importance of relationships were particularly memorable. I want you to know that you have changed the lives of 40 of my students. Thank you!"

Joanne W. (Singapore Workshop Attendee)

* * *

"...We will be inviting Rob back on every possible occasion to work with all of our participants and trainees."

"We were delighted to be able to get Rob Plevin in to work with our Teach First participants. From the start his dynamic approach captivated the group and they were enthralled throughout. Rob covered crucial issues relating to behaviour management thoroughly and worked wonders in addressing the participants' concerns about teaching in some of the most challenging schools in the country. We will be inviting Rob back on every possible occasion to work with all of our participants and trainees."

Terry Hudson, (Regional Director 'Teach First', Sheffield Hallam University)

* * *

"Thank you for helping me to be in more control."

"Rob, thank you very much for sharing your experience and reminding of these simple but effective things to do. Students' behaviour (or actually my inability to control it) is so frustrating that at times it feels that nothing can help. Thank you for helping me to be in more control."

Natasha Grydasova (_Take Control of the Noisy Class_ customer)

* * *

"I am HAPPILY spending my Sat afternoon listening, watching and reading all your extremely helpful information!"

"Thank You Rob! What a wealth of excellent ideas! This is my 30th year teaching! You would think after 30 years teaching that I wouldn't need to be viewing your awesome videos and reading your helpful blog and website. However, I am HAPPILY spending my Sat afternoon listening, watching and reading all your extremely helpful information! Thank You So Much! I will be one of your biggest fans from now on!"

Kelly Turk (Needs Focused Video Pack customer)

* * *

"...terrific for those teachers who are frustrated."

"Great easy-to-listen-to video tips that will be terrific for those teachers who are frustrated.

I'm forwarding this email on to the principals in my district right away!"

Sumner price (Take Control of the Noisy Class customer)

* * *

"Many thanks for all these really helpful life-savers!"

"Very many thanks. I have given myself trouble by letting kids into the room in a restless state with inevitable waste of teaching time. Your advice on calming them down in a positive, non-confrontational way and building rapport is very timely. Many thanks for all these really helpful life-savers!"

Philip Rozario (Take Control of the Noisy Class customer)

* * *

"Fantastic way to create a calm and secure learning environment for all the students."

"Thanks so much Rob. Fantastic way to create a calm and secure learning environment for all the students. It's great how you model the way we should interact with the students – firmly but always with respect."

Marion (Take Control of the Noisy Class customer)

* * *

"I will be recommending that the teachers in training that I deal with should have a look at these videos."

These tips and hints are put in a really clear, accessible fashion. As coordinator of student teachers in my school, I will be recommending that the teachers in training that I deal with should have a look at these videos.

Deb (Take Control of the Noisy Class customer)

* * *

"I found Rob Plevin's workshop just in time to save me from giving up."

"I found Rob Plevin's workshop just in time to save me from giving up. It should be compulsory – everybody in teaching should attend a Needs-Focused workshop and meet the man with such a big heart who will make you see the important part you can play in the lives of your most difficult students."

Heather Beames (Workshop Attendee)

* * *

"...the ideas, strategies and routines shared with our teachers have led to improved classroom practice."

"The Needs Focused Behaviour Management workshops in support of teacher training in Northern Ireland have been very well received and the ideas, strategies and routines shared with our teachers have led to improved classroom practice. This has been validated by both inspections at the University and observations of teachers."

Celia O'Hagan, (PGCE Course Leader, School of Education, University of Ulster)

* * *

"I have never enjoyed a course, nor learnt as much as I did with Rob."

"What a wonderfully insightful, non-patronising, entertainingly informative day. I have never enjoyed a course, nor learnt as much as I did with Rob. I was so impressed that I am recommending our school invite Rob along to present to all the staff so that we can all benefit from his knowledge, experience and humour."

Richard Lawson-Ellis (Workshop Attendee)

* * *

"...since I started following the principles in your materials, I have seen a vast improvement."

"Hi Rob, I would just like to say that since I started following the principles in your materials, I have seen a vast improvement. I had to teach a one hour interview lesson yesterday and was told that they thought the lesson was super and they loved my enthusiasm! I got the job!

Diane Greene (_Take Control of the Noisy Class customer_)

* * *

"Thanks to you, students from 30 some schools are truly engaged and not throwing pencils at the sub!"

Rob, Your student engagement series has been out of this world. I've already used various techniques as a substitute and students said I was **the best sub ever.** Thanks to you, students from 30 some schools are truly engaged and not throwing pencils at the sub!"

Leslie Mueller (Student Engagement Formula customer)

* * *

"So often professional development training is a waste of time; you may get one little gem from a whole day of training. You've given numerous strategies in 5 minutes."

Wow! So many people have gained so much from your videos! Teachers are time poor. A quick grab of effective ideas is what we all need. So often professional development training is a waste of time; you may get one little gem from a whole day of training. You've given numerous strategies in 5 minutes. Thanks for your generosity.

Mary – Ann (Take Control of the Noisy Class customer)

Strategies List

Made in the USA
Las Vegas, NV
22 March 2023

69505301R00080